The Church and the Suburbs

The Church and the schools

THE
CHURCH
AND THE
SUBURBS

by Andrew M. Greeley

(Revised Edition)

DEUS BOOKS
PAULIST PRESS
(Paulist Fathers)
New York, N. Y.

*The reason we fly from the city is not
that it is not poetical; it is that
its poetry is too fierce, too fascinating
and too practical in its demands.*

G. K. CHESTERTON

FOR THE YOUNG PEOPLE OF
CHRIST THE KING PARISH

A Deus Books Edition of the Paulist Press, 1963, by special
arrangement with Sheed & Ward, Inc., New York, N. Y.

NIHIL OBSTAT: Reynold Hillenbrand, *Censor Deputatus*

IMPRIMATUR: ✠ Albert G. Meyer, *Archbishop of Chicago*

Chicago, June 8, 1959

Contents

INTRODUCTION   7

AUTHOR'S PREFACE   9

PREFACE TO REVISED EDITION   13

I. THE SUBURBAN EXPANSION   14

   1. Are Suburbs Necessary?   15

   2. The Changing City   25

   3. Suburbia: The "Good" Life   35

II. THE CHURCH AND THE SUBURBS   44

   4. The Suburban Revival   45

   5. The Catholic Suburbanite   53

   6. The Suburban Parish   62

   7. The Suburban Priest   71

   8. The Parish as a Community   77

III. THE FAMILY AND THE SUBURBS   86

   9. The Suburban Husband—
      The Vanishing American   87

  10. The Suburban Wife—Who Needs Her?   97

  11. The Young People of Suburbia—
      Not Exactly "Shook-Up"   106

IV. SUBURBAN HUMANISM   115

    12. Conformity or Community   116

    13. The Waning of Enthusiasm   125

    14. Beat, Cool—and Lonely   135

    15. Permanent Prosperity?   142

    16. Leisure and Popular Culture   149

    17. Program for Oblivion   157

V. THE SUBURBAN APOSTOLATE   162

    18. Popular Culture and the Roman Rite   163

    19. The New Social Action   172

    20. A Spirituality for Suburbanites   180

    21. Conclusion   188

Introduction

The mass movement to the suburbs is one of the factors which is contributing to a significant change in the American way life. Sociologists, educators and businessmen have made studies of this modern phenomenon with an eye to its implications in their respective fields. The Church, too, is deeply involved in the move to Suburbia. New Parishes are being created in places which a short time ago were farms or open fields. Pastors are facing the problem of providing schools for vast numbers of children and building churches which are sometimes too small for the growing population by the time they are finished.

This presents a real problem for the diocese. Priests must be shifted about in order to meet the needs of the shifting population. Somehow the new communities must be served without neglecting the old parishes in the heart of the city, which in many cases are becoming missionary territory. The financial problems which the Church has to face because of this new phenomenon are great. The spiritual problems which it presents are even greater and much more subtle. The suburban life seems to be pleasant and prosperous. Is it too pleasant and to prosperous to be compatible with the truly Christian life?

On the other hand, the new suburbanite is usually a regular churchgoer. Does this mean a deeper religious life made possible by favorable circumstances? Suburbanites know their neighbors to an extent which they never did in the city. They take a greater interest in all the activities of the community. Does this give promise of the formation of a Christian community in the suburbs? Is religion in the suburbs the real thing or merely the fashionable thing? These are some of the questions which we must ask ourselves as Catholics viewing the present scene.

Father Andrew Greely has been for the past five years an assistant in a parish which is located within the limits of the city but which has many of the aspects of a suburban parish. He is intensely active in parish work—the work of teaching, instructing converts, administering the sacraments, youth work, athletic programs, counseling — all the manifold and varied work of a parish priest. He has been active in promoting participation in the liturgy in the parish to which he is assigned, and is chaplain to both Young Christian Student and Christian Family Movement groups. This background of parish work, coupled with a natural ability in religious sociology, has given him an insight into the problem of suburban Catholicism. He has been interested in the subject since his seminary days, and has been studying and writing about it for several years. Somehow he has been able to combine this study and writing with his strenuous schedule of parish work. In fact, it is probably precisely because he has been able to make this sucessful combination that he is so well qualified to write this book. Every page reveals that this is no mere theorizing on a problem which has been studied in books. It is based on experience in working within the situation. It is my belief that this book will help throw real light on a problem which concerns all Catholics and everyone who is interested in the future development of the Church in the United States.

MSGR. EDWARD M. BURKE, P.A.
CHANCELLOR
ARCHDIOCESE OF CHICAGO

Author's Preface

A writer undergoes a considerable risk when he attempts to write about the suburbs. Not only is the subject so complicated that even the most timid generalization always has an exception, but it has also, for some unaccountable reason, become controversial. As a result, one who reports on the suburbs is expected to take a stand. Suburbia is in the same class as the labor movement; one is constrained to be for it or against it. It is a somewhat dismal consideration to suspect that when a book on the suburbs is put down, the reader will feel every right to say with triumph, "He's for them," or, with equal triumph, "He's against them."

So it should be noted at the beginning that this book about Suburbia is neither for nor against Suburbia. I am a suburbanite by birth, rearing, and assignment. I am fully aware that suburban Catholicism is impressive, that suburban parishes are active, dedicated organizations, and that suburban Catholics are sending their children to seminaries and convents in remarkable numbers. I further realize that the material affluence of the suburbs represents a remarkable triumph over poverty and misery. These vast areas of brightness in the suburban picture are mentioned in their proper place in this volume. If they are not emphasized as much as are some of the darker aspects of the same picture, it is not because they are thought to be unimportant or irrelevant, but merely because the purpose of the book is not to pay compliments or describe happy living, but rather to ask questions and pose problems.

There are many things which this book is not. It

can make no claim to be a scientific study of suburban life. Suburbia is a vast, complex and relatively new phenomenon, and scientific studies of it are still in their infancy. This book, while based on the scientific information available, is an exploratory inquiry which will attempt to point out only some of the main suburban problems and their implication for the Catholic Church.

Nor can the book claim to be a work of professional sociology. I am not a sociologist but a parish priest. The essays collected in this volume are the result of personal experience, of reflection, reading and discussion. They are, then, merely an attempt to report one priest's impressions of the suburban migration.

Finally, the book is in no sense of the word comprehensive. A more accurate subtitle might be "The Church and some Suburban Problems." Only certain aspects of the suburban trend are discussed; others are merely alluded to in passing and some are hardly mentioned. For example, much more could have been said about metropolitan planning and regional zoning. However, I know very little about this subject and information on it is not readily accessible. Nor is there much reference to the staggering problem of building Catholic schools for the suburban younger generation. Even an informal treatment of all the important facets of suburban life would take a volume many times the size of this one.

It may well be objected that I ask many questions but provide few answers. If there is a shortage of answers in this book, the principal reason is that I don't know the answers, in many cases not even the beginnings of answers. At this stage of the development of what I will call suburban humanism, it seems that merely asking certain questions might be of some service. My purpose is to attempt to begin discussion, not to attempt to end it.

In the third chapter we distinguish between the blue-collar suburb and the white-collar suburb—or, more accurately, between the upper middle class and the lower middle class. It is almost inevitable that the type of suburb and suburbanite described in this book will be more white collar than blue. Most of the suburbs that have been the objects of study belong in the former class. Even though the blue-collar area is an extremely important one, we still know rather little about it. However, it would seem that the white-collar areas are setting the whole tone of suburban life, and hence the emphasis placed on them in this book might not be altogether unwarranted.

As should be obvious from several of the chapters, the problems of the suburbs cannot be isolated from those of the central city. To focus on suburban life does not mean that there are not other areas of concern for the Catholic Church in the United States. It does not even necessarily mean that Suburbia is the most important area in which the Church should be interested. But it does mean that if the American Church does not effectively adjust itself to the new suburban humanism, it will have an increasingly difficult task in the years to come.

I must express my gratitude to the people who have assisted in various ways in the writing of this book: Msgr. Edward M. Burke, P.A., for his encouragement and his gracious Foreword; to Msgrs. Wm. Quinn, John Egan and George Higgins for their many helpful comments; to Fathers Gerard Weber, John Krump, Walter Imbiorski, J. Michael Hartnett, Patrick Ronayne, James Kilgallon and Edmund Fitzpatrick for their valuable criticisms; to my fellow priests at Christ the King, Msgr. P. J. Gleeson, and Fathers Warren McCarthy and John McAvoy for listening patiently to my theories (even though, it should be noted, this book is in no sense a description of the parish); to several couples from the Christian Family Movement who have had many penetrating suggestions—Dick and Gerry Roche, Frank and Rita Doubeck, Bob and Corrine Podesta, Ed and Cyrila Power, Jim and Mercedes Smith, Don and Ann O'Brien; and finally to a delightfully untypical group of young suburbanites for their aid in the chapters on suburban youth and on enthusiasm — Thomas Brennan, James Casey, Richard Kelly, Robert Burke, Patrick Brennan, Robert Kopecky, Helen Hunt and Mary Ellen Podesta.

Grateful acknowledgment is made to the editors of *The Sign, Worship, Ave Maria, The Catholic World, Worship* and *America* for permission to reprint material which first appeared in their pages.

I regret that in a few instances I have been unable to recall the publications which were the sources of brief comments quoted in this book.

MARCH 10, 1959

Preface to *Revised Edition*

When an author prepares a book for a second edition, it is fashionable for him to assert that of course his ideas have developed considerably since he first wrote the work, but he reissues the book in its original form because of its historic value. I must admit that there are not too many changes in this edition: one new chapter (Chapter 8), one paragraph omitted (the charge made is no longer true), one paragraph added, three new footnotes and the dropping of the title "Senator" from the name of John Kennedy.

The reason for the scarcity of modifications is not that I have any illusion that the preservation of my thought in its 1959 state has any historic value. But the passage of the years has not caused me to change my mind on the problems discussed.

The problems of suburbia are very much with us still and the answers are as elusive as ever. In retrospect, I wish I had made it clearer that the suburbia I was talking about was the white-collar suburb. However, there has been only one study which, to my knowledge (Berger's *Working Class Suburb*), considers the blue-collar suburb; as far as I can determine its findings are inconclusive. The absence of material in this volume on working class suburbs is not due to any estimation that they are unimportant. Rather, I suspect that they are an extremely significant aspect of American life. We say nothing about them for the same reason as in the first edition: we do not know much about them.

I offer no apology for the absence of solutions. When an author poses questions, his only obligation is to make the questions as clear as possible; ready-made solutions are a cheap delusion. The original purpose of this volume was to begin discussion which might some day lead to tentative solutions. The purpose is substantially unchanged.   AUGUST 2, 1962

I. The Suburban Expansion

Suburbia is both a place and a way of life. The first chapter describes the background of urban expansion against which the suburban drama is being enacted. The second chapter examines Suburbia as a physical phenomenon; the third outlines the problems besetting the suburban psyche.

1
Are
Suburbs
Necessary?

The suburbs, it would appear, are here to stay. They may be a necessary evil, they may be the beginning of a new era of human freedom and dignity. But, short of a nuclear war, they are likely to be an expanding figure in the American countryside for many decades to come. The forest of TV aerials, the gaping picture windows along the expressway, are so taken for granted in this second half of the twentieth century that few people have bothered to ask why. In an industrial society it is certainly inevitable that big cities will grow, but it is not at all inevitable that they will grow in the form they have taken in America. Suburbs are not an absolutely necessary result of urban expansion. LeCorbusier, the famed French architect, many years ago made an excellent theoretical case for *La Ville Radieuse,* an urban metropolis of giant skyscraper apartments occupying much less land than present cities. Such a city would be more orderly and much more convenient than our present sprawling urban regions. It would also have spared our countryside the ravages of suburban blight.

La Ville Radieuse never had a chance. Very few of us would have wanted to live in it, despite its neat architectural lines and blindingly rational plan. However, it represented an alternative. There is no reason, in the nature of things, why much of our postwar suburban expansion (from twenty million to forty million inhabitants, with an estimate of perhaps sixty million by 1970) could not have been in apartment houses instead of single-family dwellings. It

15

might in the long run have been much more convenient and economical. If we are fully to understand
the social and psychological problems involved in
suburban living, we must investigate what the social
and psychological reasons are for the surburban explosion.

What, in the first place, is a suburb? It is something more than a place beyond the city limits. The
boundaries of cities are normally very accidental and
haphazard lines. Two practically identical neighborhoods may face each other across the city limits.
Technically and legally, one may be a suburb and
another not. But in culture and psychology they are
almost the same. They are the result of the same
trends in American life and pose the same problems
for the planner, the psychiatrist and the clergyman.
Suburbia is not merely a legal entity; it is a way of
life and a state of mind. It is to this way of life and
this state of mind that this chapter (and this book)
addresses itself.

The skilled market analysts of *Fortune* defined as
suburban any census tract in a metropolitan area in
which two-thirds of the families owned their own
homes and in which both the income and the number of children were above the national average. By
these standards there were at the time of the *Fortune*
Survey (1954) some seven million homes in these
suburban tracts. Most of them were beyond the city
limits, but some were within the legal boundaries of
cities. The precise definitions of a suburb are a matter of some importance for sociologists, market re-
searchers and the Bureau of Census; but the average
person, while he may have some difficulty in judging
whether a given neighborhood could be called suburban or not, thinks of Suburbia mainly as the sprawling area of single-family residences on the fringe of
the city.

Although a considerable amount of ink has been

consumed in books and articles about suburbs since the end of the Second World War, the suburbs are by no means a new phenomenon in American society. The isolated pioneer studies made in the 1920's and 1930's show that the forces at work in the post-war suburban expansion were at work as long as forty years ago. Indeed a book like H. P. Douglass' *The Suburban Trend,* although written in the early 1920's, might just as well have been published last year. His suburbs differ very little either physically or culturally from ours. It would seem that even the suburban religious revival was well on its way at the time of his book. It would take considerable study to document this notion with certainty, but it seems possible that Suburbia as a goal and a cultural force has been operating in America since the beginning of the century. The tremendous expansion after the last war was only partially caused by factors peculiar to the post-war world. The Depression and the war may have merely retarded a growth which would have taken place anyhow. The suburban expansion of the 1940's and '50's would seem to be the nation's attempt to make up for lost time, to accomplish the growth which was denied it in the '30's.

The most obvious explanation for the suburban urge is simply that an expanding city needs land and that there was and is a considerable amount of land available at the fringe of urban development. So the development continues in a series of concentric circles, first along the main arteries of transportation, then filling up the gaps in between the arteries. Even if there is a considerable amount of vacant land within the built-up area, this land is either undesirable (too close to factories or dumping land) or uneconomical for construction purposes. For if a "developer" is to make his usually considerable profit, he must be able to use what passes in the construction industry for mass production. That means he must be able to lay anywhere from fifty to twenty-five hundred practically identical foundations in a limited area and then, without too much moving around, construct the same number of practically identical frames on these foundations. It is not worth his money to worry about building up the many isolated vacant lots or small tracts still available within the central city.

While many of those engaged in the real estate or construction professions yield to no one in their cupidity, it is probably unfair to blame them for the suburban expansion. Their "developments" would not have been purchased before construction was completed unless there were other factors at work creating a demand for *anything* that could be called a home.

Most Americans seem driven to have a place they can call a home of their own. Apartment living just does not seem right to a good portion of our society. The high rents of recent years, plus the low payments made possible by the Federal Housing Authority and the Veterans' Administration, have given extra force to the desire for four walls that a person can think of as "home sweet home." As individuals and as a nation we found it exceedingly natural, when faced with the housing shortage of the 1940's, to stack the deck in favor of the single-family dwelling. Mixing our national metaphors, we went on an orgy of pulling up stakes so that we could sink roots. The hectic prosperity of the years after the war made it possible for our suburban dream to come true, much to the delight of the real estate and construction men, obstetricians, and manufacturers of barbecue pits. The gray hairs on the heads of city planners, traffic engineers, suburban pastors, and lovers of the beauty of rural America were a necessary part of the price.

But the stubborn question persists: Why does the vast American middle class so ardently desire homes of its own, even though the cost is often prohibitive? The automobile is a big help, of course; it makes it possible to cover the ever increasing distances between home and work. However, the gasoline engine has, to some extent, defeated itself. With automobile ownership doubling every decade or so (present total, sixty million) and expressway construction lagging far behind, suburban transportation is getting worse instead of better, but the construction of new developments continues on its merry way. The automobile has put self-owned transportation at the disposal of a far higher proportion of Americans than fifty years ago; but it has not noticeably increased their safety, peace of mind or, in some cases, even speed in transit.

Physical and mechanical factors have indeed been at work in this "every man with his own castle" craze, but the deepest cause of the growth of Suburbia is a longing of the human spirit. The suburb represents certain values to which most Americans feel they have some sort of right. It represents the culmination of the Good Life for which we all have the privilege of striving. Suburban bliss is one of the ends of the American success story. In fact, in this day of "enjoy now, pay later," the suburban dream need not be the end of successful striving, but only the beginning.

The suburb is, first of all, the place to raise a family. It has become part of our thinking that apartment houses and crowded city streets breed delinquency and that the more natural wide-open spaces of the countryside are far better suited to the normal and healthy development of children. The suburb is supposed to be a happy compromise between the bliss of the countryside and the convenience of the city. Not only does the suburbanite justify his move by saying it is for the good of his wife and children; he uses the same argument to explain the country club membership, the barbecue pit, and even the swimming pool in the back yard. The psychology is little different from that of the father who buys an electric train for his son at Christmas and then monopolizes its use.

It is indeed open to question whether the child-centeredness of our present society is not a form of escapism in which the parent identifies himself with the simpler pleasures of childhood and thus recaptures the dreams of his own lost youth. Whatever the subconscious explanations, the desire to do everything possible for one's children is a strong motive for moving to the suburbs. Objectively, of course, it is questionable whether delinquency is the result of location or of family instability and social class, but such considerations seldom occur to the person with his eye on a "place in the suburbs."

For the suburbs are more than just a place to raise children; they are also a place where one can "enjoy life." The grimy, gloomy city with its hustle and bustle is dedicated to the process of making a living, but in the suburb one can begin to take some pleasure from the fruits of one's efforts. Golf, gardening, bridge clubs, casual clothes, landscaped lawns, gaily colored houses—all these make the suburbanite's life look like one long vacation. The suburbanite is surrounded by all sorts of indoor gadgets for saving time and outdoor gadgets for spending it. Hence he can "relax a little and have some fun." In the Anglo-Saxon world there has been a long tradition of leisurely and gracious country living for the affluent class. In our age of Affluence for Everyman the suburban home gives the average citizen his own manor house, his own country estate. In an upwardly mobile population the suburban home is a symbol of status. Its owner has "arrived," and he can settle down to enjoying the results of his success—whether he wants to or not.

He may possibly be in for some disillusionment.

Gardening might not be nearly as much fun as it looked in the city. As one frustrated suburban housewife told a University of Chicago interviewer, "I really hate gardening; we both do. My husband never plays golf any more, and we do nothing all week-end but work in the garden. I mean '*work*.'" If the garden is a status symbol, there is no better way to lose status than by letting the garden run down. The more insecure the status, the more effort is demanded in maintaining the external appearances of the manor house. Hence in the so-called blue-collar suburbs, not to keep up with one's neighbors in arraying one's home and lot is a major offense, to be punished by social ostracism.

Furthermore, as Robert Wood has pointed out recently,[1] the American political image of the small town as being the basic unit in grass roots democracy has played a part in suburban expansion. Since the time of the New England town meetings, there has always lurked in some corner of the American mind the notion that real democratic government and hence real Americanism are possible only in small towns. The pseudo-small town which a suburb is appeals to the American longing for an honest, manageable local government in which everyone can participate and which in some fashion is our republic in miniature.

The suburb is, finally, a place to which one can belong. "Togetherness," as we will say elsewhere in this book, is not merely a fad. It represents modern man's attempt to regain some of that community which his ancestors had in the peasant society of Europe or the frontier society of nineteenth-century America. Several different surveys indicate that suburbanites seem to have a higher level of need for friendship, community participation, and a sense of belonging. In a

[1] *Suburbia: Its People and Their Politics* (Boston: Houghton Mifflin, 1959), pp. 5-20.

rootless society the suburb is a place to sink roots. In a meaningless culture, the suburban community is a place to find significance. In an unfriendly and anonymous civilization, the suburb is a place which offers friendliness and room for individual development.

Suburbia is, in short, an escape from industrialism. The suburbanite wants to enjoy the fruits of industrial society without paying all of its cost. He wants to escape from the ugly, complicated city to the pastoral simplicity of the country. The suburb is a way-station on this escape. Despite the claims of city planners that ideal communities should be a mixture of occupational and residential sections, modern urban land use is becoming more and more specialized. In our attempt to escape from the factory we are devoting certain land areas to the blight of industrial production, and other land areas (farther and farther away) to dormitory space. Despite the fact that there is considerable industrial expansion at the fringe of the city, the satellite suburb (the suburb with some industry of its own) is growing much less rapidly than the pure dormitory suburb. The suburb, then, is the city's attempt to outgrow itself—an attempt which unfortunately seems doomed to failure.

For the suburbs are still part of the big city, whether they like it or not. They are not and never will be rural; on the contrary, they are urban fragments, places where certain specialized aspects of urban living take place, dependent on but isolated from other urban activities. As long ago as 1921 Lewis Mumford observed, "The commuter who spends a good deal of his day wandering . . . between heaven and hell presents a spectacle much more humiliating than a man without a country; he is a man without a city—in short, a barbarian. Small wonder that bathtubs and heating systems and similar apparatus play such a large part in his conception of the good life. In our modern cities, we have built Suburbia, which is a common refuge from life, and the remedy is worse than the disease."

And Henry Hope Reed comments: "Too often we forget that the suburb has been built at a terrifying cost. This lies not primarily in the loss of the country-side before the lengthening superhighway and the spreading development; that is perhaps inevitable in the face of a growing population and the very natural desire of the American to own his home. Rather it lies in the abandonment of the city, the center of our civilization. Like the mad hatter at the tea party who moved around the table using only the clean cups and leaving the dirty ones behind him, we Americans move to new land once we have exploited the old. The central city has seemingly been worked for all that it is worth and then abandoned for the suburban fringe. What is perhaps more frightening is that the suburban fringe of 25 or 15 years ago is in its turn being worn out." [2]

So the city is working vengeance on those who deserted it. Neither physically nor psychologically can it be escaped. As if to prove the city's power, urban blight spreads like wildfire through the new developments. What was yesterday's dream house becomes a building in today's conservation neighborhood and tomorrow's slum. In fact, some of the new suburbs are slums almost as soon as the first foundation is poured. The flight from industrialism has proved to be an impossible cause. The suburban vision is rapidly fading into a nightmare world of rocky streets, flooded basements, overcrowded schools and peeling paint.

Yet the suburban vision is still a valid one. The desires for home, community, leisure, and beauty are natural and good. That they have been only partially realized in the suburbs can be attributed to many fac-

[2] Henry Hope Reed and Christopher Tunnard, *American Skyline* (Boston: Houghton Mifflin, 1955).

tors — greed, political and planning incompetence, narrowness, apathy. However, the basic weakness of the contemporary suburban vision is the notion that industrial man can achieve these desirable human goals without reforming industrialism. The suburban escape has partially failed precisely because it was an escape. The division between city and suburb is largely a myth. The suburb is just a different part of the city.

The suburbanite will escape the frustrations and disappointments of his new life only when he realizes that suburbs cannot be satisfying places to live until the whole metropolitan region has begun to be a satisfying place. The suburbanite might not like it, but he is still an inhabitant of the big city and must face its problems. If he does not, then the development of metropolitan America must be left to the modern robber barons, and our descendants will feel about us as we do about those apathetic forefathers of ours who permitted the destruction of our forests and pasture lands. Suburbia could be one of the best things that has happened to our nation—the beginning of a new humanism; but it could also be the beginning of one of our worst national disasters.

Against this somber backdrop we will examine in the next chapter the changing city from which the suburbanite has attempted to flee.

2
The
Changing
City

A curious and almost frightening aspect of American life is the rapidity with which words lose their meaning. Our country is changing so quickly that a word can have an entirely different meaning today from that of twenty years ago. A classic example of this mobility of language can be found in the use of the words "city," "suburb," and "country." Twenty years ago the meanings of these words were quite clear. A city contained a central business district, an industrial area, slums, and then gradually improving residential neighborhoods. Around the city limits there were clustered a few suburbs which were little more than a continuation of the final neighborhood belt in the city. Beyond the suburbs was the countryside—farms, forest, pasture. The distinction was simple and neat; no one hesitated to use the words. But today all is changed. The suburbs are becoming urban; the countryside is being engulfed by suburbs; and the whole nation is rapidly becoming one gigantic city.

This is not an exaggeration. Even now we have huge metropolitan "strips" stretching for hundreds of miles and containing tens of millions of residents. In a few decades, we are told, such strips will extend from Boston to Newport News to Toledo, from Milwaukee to Fort Wayne and from San Francisco to Tia Juana. The emergence of these gigantic supercities, crazy-quilt mixtures of city and suburbs, of slum and factory, ranch house and shopping plaza, expressway and skyscraper, is probably the most significant social fact of our era and one which poses many problems for the Catholic Church.

The causes of this spectacular growth of cities and the problems resulting from it are mixed together in such a tangled and complicated web that it is extremely difficult to discuss the various factors in orderly fashion. Yet the implications of the "super-city" are so vast and so important that every American must make an effort to understand what is at stake before it is too late.

The "super-city" is the result in great part of the mammoth post-war industrial boom. The American economy stood still for almost a decade during the Great Depression, and civilian needs were shunted off during the war years. But from 1946 on, American production increased at a fantastic rate. Old industries expanded more than anyone believed possible and new industries appeared almost overnight. New factories sprang up and old factories were remodeled and replaced. Since most modern companies depend on other companies for their supplies or distribution, it was natural that sites should be selected near already existing facilities. Hence the big cities and the areas around them became the focal point of the postwar boom. Industry grew, population skyrocketed, the suburbs sprawled out into the countryside and the super-city was born.

The problems connected with this growth of metropolitan regions are many, but three stand out above all the others—immigration, housing and planning.

Despite the many inventions grouped under the general heading of "automation," a spectacular spurt in production still involves an increase in the demand for labor. Except for the three brief recessions in the last decade and a half, the labor supply has always been short. Hence the needs of this boom, like those of most previous booms in our country's history, must be met by immigration. In the past it was the Germans and Scandinavians, then the Irish, then the Poles, then the Italians who met the demand for workers. Today, however, our immigration laws made it impossible for us to look to foreign countries for our labor supply; hence we must search about within our own borders for the new immigrants. Recruiters must look for workers within the country instead of abroad as they did in former years. They have found that there are still three sources of cheap labor available—the Negroes, the Spanish-speaking (Puerto Ricans and Mexicans), and the Country Folk ("Southern Whites," or "hill-billies").

The problems of the New Immigrants are in many ways similar to the difficulties which the Old Immigrants faced. It is quite interesting to compare the anti-Irish publications of seventy-five years ago with the anti-Negro publications of today. The Yankee Protestants viewed the Irish immigrants with the same fear and contempt with which some of the descendants of these immigrants view the newer arrivals. The modern immigrants, like the ones of yesteryear, are predominantly rural people, suddenly put at the mercy of a complex and hectic urban culture for which they have no preparation. Their family life disintegrates, crime and delinquency abound in their neighborhoods, they find their recreation in drink, narcotics (a problem that earlier groups did not have) and street fights. They are at the mercy of clever politicians and unscrupulous businessmen and labor leaders. The larger community looks on their manners as uncouth and their morals as atrocious. They are discriminated against at every turn and are the objects of fear, contempt and hatred. They are poorly fed, poorly housed, poorly clothed. They are perhaps making more money than they did in their former homes, but they may be far more miserable.

It should be obvious to any intelligent person that these people are not racially inferior to those who came before them. They are simply uneducated and unskilled in the ways of what passes for civilization in the big city. The process of getting used to city life (what the sociologists would call "acculturation") is bound to take time—perhaps a generation or two. However, in the case of the new immigrants there are factors which tend to slow down acculturation. The Negroes and the Spanish-speaking not only have to face the normal discrimination leveled at any immigrant group, they are also the object of a racial prejudice which will reject them even if they learn city ways. The Country Folk, on the other hand, refuse to consider themselves as a minority group, and with stubborn pride and independence oppose any attempts at education or organization. It is indeed a strange irony of modern urban culture that the descendants of the yeomanry who defeated the British one hundred and seventy-five years ago can now be treated as the most despised of newcomers.

For the Negro group there is the additional problem that the traumatic slavery experience has deprived them of the family life and community organizational skills which many of the other ethnic groups brought to the new world. The way up the ladder is harder for the Negro not only because of his skin color but because his recent past has left him a man virtually without a culture or a community.

The implications for the Church in this New Migration are almost frightening. A whole new mission field has opened up in the back yard of the big city dioceses. Hundreds of thousands of potential converts are crammed into the slums where the immigrants are settling. The Church fortunately has mission stations already built. Large parish plants, once the centers of thriving Catholic communities, have grown empty and silent as the Catholic population moved away; but some of them have begun to take on new life as missionary parishes. The transition is hard on the priests and hard on the diocese, but progress is being made. Some parishes in the Negro neighborhoods have taken on much of their former vigor. Organizations like New York's Spanish Catholic Action and Chicago's Committee for the Spanish-speaking are beginning to make clear to the Puerto Ricans that, despite the immense difference in appearances, the Catholic Church here is the same as that which they left behind in their native lands. With the Southern Whites the obstacles are much greater. They view the Church of Rome with the same distrust and suspicion that their forefathers showed in the eighteenth century. Catholic progress among the Country Folk has been limited indeed.

For the Catholic these new immigrants are more than just people to be converted. Virtually all the corporal and spiritual works of mercy come into play in helping these confused newcomers adjust to city life. For the Catholic laity, and particularly the newly well-to-do in the suburbs, the migrant groups present an accusing challenge.

Closely connected to the problem of immigration is the housing situation. Americans may be the best-housed people in the world, and yet a good portion of our population lives in conditions that are inadequate and indefensible. From 1930 to 1945 there was virtually no residential home building. By the end of World War II there were millions of substandard units. The tremendous building boom of the post-war era eased the situation somewhat, but most of the slums still remain and have been joined by the ready-made suburban slum of the wooden-box-on-a-concrete-slab variety. The influx of the New Immigrants has created housing pressures from the center of the city far out into the area where suburban construction blends into countryside. As a result, poor housing and slums are now no longer limited to the heart of the metropolitan area but run through the whole of the super-city like a cancerous growth. Some of the worst slums in the country are the "temporary" veterans' housing projects of the mid-forties; and some of the dreariest places on the face of the continent are the public housing projects erected as part of "slum clearance" programs.

To add to the anomaly of the spreading slums, the ugliest kind of blight can often be found side by side with the most exclusive residential suburb. Real estate speculators are often interested only in getting a development up; what happens to a charming countryside matters very little. The Maryland hills north of Washington, New York's Westchester County and Long Island, Illinois's Fox River Valley and many other lovely sections relatively close to big cities are in danger of being converted into one great hodgepodge of residential and industrial developments where the span from countryside to blight can be covered in less than one generation.

The destruction of beauty by slums——old or new—may seem a small matter when compared with the overcrowding and poor sanitation of the old slums. The obliteration of a lovely vista may seem a small price to pay for the building of a new home. The grim skyscrapers or the public and semi-public housing, even if they are like penal institutions or above-ground bomb shelters, may be thought to be better than nothing. But these are not necessary alternatives. In a society with our resources it is not necessary to be content with structural solidity and efficient sewage disposal.

There are those who think that more and better housing is the greatest single social need in our country. The increase in marriages, the baby boom, the new migrations certainly make the housing problem acute. Some progress has been made in the last decade, but it has been at a high cost in financial, natural, and human resources. If "muddling through" continues to be the philosophy of the nation's housing policy, the result for the super-city is going to be disastrous.

The Church's stake in better housing is clear enough. The connection between adequate housing and decent family life is so obvious that no one questions it. A slum parish is normally a bad parish—financially and spiritually. The pell-mell growth of the super-city is costing the Church a fortune. As neighborhoods become blighted before their time, parishes become deserted and schools empty almost overnight. The process of converting the immigrant groups would be much easier if vigorous parishes did not collapse all at once. On the fringe of the city new parishes can turn into suburban slums during the lifetime of their founding pastor. Nor can the Church, which for many years was the custodian of most of what is beautiful in Western civilization, look with indifference on the ruination of much of the beauty of God's natural creation in the American countryside.

Some Catholic efforts are being devoted to the housing problem. The priests engaged in social action work have been hammering at poor housing for more than a quarter of a century. Some large dioceses have conservation committees which try to arrest the progress of blight in the old neighborhoods of the city. Many urban parishes co-operate with the neighborhood improvement associations in trying to safeguard the community from the forces that would turn it into a slum. Some Catholic Action groups are more and more active in this neighborhood conservation work. Unfortunately, neighborhood "improvement" often becomes little more than a last-ditch effort to keep the new immigrants out. Intelligent participation by the Catholic laity in community efforts to obtain satisfactory housing is still quite small.

A third problem of the super-city is planning. The

fantastic expansion of the metropolis is something that can no longer be left to chance. The vast industrial and economic forces at work within and around the urban center must be in some sort of harmony if utter chaos is not to result. City planning is not a particularly new science, but the magnitude of the problems it faces is new and its efforts to date in the super-city leave something to be desired.

There are at least three separate elements in city planning — renewal of deteriorated neighborhoods, conservation of threatened neighborhoods and expansion of the metropolitan area. Various projects—such as the construction of expressways — are part of all three. Each aspect of city planning has its own special set of obstacles.

Renewal work always gets a considerable amount of publicity in city newspapers. Vast new housing projects in place of slums, expensive housing in badly blighted areas, shopping centers, parking lots, convention halls, new highways — all these make excellent copy for the press. Much good work has been done in this rebuilding of the center of the city, and much more needs to be done if the heart of the metropolitan region is to be saved from death by strangulation.

Nevertheless, there are many criticisms of these projects which seldom if ever get into the press. Often they are pushed ahead with little or no consideration for the local community or the problems of the city as a whole. It may be all well and good to build a series of new skyscraper apartments in badly deteriorated neighborhoods. But if thousands of people are dispossessed of their dwellings without adequate provisions being made for other housing, then the result of the new project will simply be to move blight from one neighborhood to another. There can be no objection to new superhighways, but if a superhighway destroys a strong neighborhood community or isolates a church from the main part of a parish, there is some reason to suspect that local interests are not being given much consideration by the planners. We do not intend to condemn all renewal programs, but it is impossible to deny that the harmonization of business and commercial interests, neighborhood stability, and the welfare of the city and region is an extremely complicated task. It is also a task which has not always been accomplished with complete success.

There has been much talk of the conservation of neighborhoods threatened with blight, but only rarely has this talk led to action which actually saved the neighborhood. Mammoth redevelopment and rapid suburban expansion have captured the public interest, but the careful, day-by-day work which is necessary for the salvation of middle-aged neighborhoods has been largely left undone. Change comes so quickly in the rapidly moving city that by the time the neighborhood is aware that it has a conservation problem it is usually too late to do very much about it. The average citizen is far more interested in escaping from the oncoming minority groups by moving to a new home in the suburbs than in saving an old neighborhood from which he always wanted to escape.

The planning and regulation of expansion is perhaps the most difficult problem of all. In this field the planner is faced with the lack of an adequate vocabulary and an even worse lack of administrative units. Our ideas of what a city is are completely out of date, and so unfortunately is what passes for city government. A city is no longer merely a set of legal boundaries approved by a state legislature. It is rather a gigantic region or cluster of cities, transcending county, state, diocesan and in a few cases even national boundaries. The problems of a city do not end at a city limit, but its authority usually does. Within the super-city there are hundreds of jealous, suspicious and competing governments, each more interested in its own sovereignty than in the good of the metropolitan region as a whole. Only a few cities, such as Toronto and Seattle, have made provisions for any kind of new government authority to correspond to the new community which is the super-city. There is no question of denying legitimate independence to the smaller local governments, but there is a problem of finding some form of regional federalism through which the smaller units of the super-city can co-operate instead of fighting one another. The difficulties are often compounded by the fact that the city is usually at the mercy of a state legislature dominated by rural areas, which is more interested in deriving tax revenue from the city than in finding a solution to urban problems. So the super-city continues its reckless growth, with suburban slums appearing all over the countryside because of the lack of regional zoning. Our country continues on its way to becoming one large metropolis and perhaps one large slum, with little consideration given to educational, recreational, or cultural values.

City planning, housing, aid to the new migrants—these are not merely areas of endeavor in which converts can be made. In fact, if a Catholic grows interested in such work merely to make converts, he will probably be a double failure—poor missionary and poor city planner. Nor is it merely a matter of safeguarding the legitimate rights of the Church, though the Church has much at stake in these fields. The problem is to make the spirit of the Gospel a living reality in the midst of the critical situations of mid-twentieth-century living. The virtues of patriotism, justice and charity demand that Catholics become involved in these complicated urban problems. To the extent that the work of Catholics in solving these problems is unselfish and disinterested, to that extent the ultimate goals of the Mystical Body will be achieved in the super-city.

3
Suburbia:
The "Good" Life

The external differences between the suburbs and the old neighborhood are obvious enough. The massive apartment buildings and the long lines of two-flat houses have given way to the ranch house or the split-level dwelling. The shopping plaza has replaced the corner delicatessen; the station wagon has succeeded the sedan; the front lawn often serves the same purpose as did once the neighborhood tavern. We see gray flannel suits on commuter trains instead of working clothes on street cars, gaping picture windows instead of drawn curtains, sport shirts instead of dress shirts, denim slacks instead of skirts, and, above all, streets swarming with children.

These externals are an indication of a deeper spiritual change which is occurring in the suburban man and which makes his way of life something new in the history of our country. Who are the people that are moving to the suburbs? Who is the suburban man and woman? How are they different from the rest of us? Or are they different at all?

The man of the suburbs is one of the twenty million people who have moved to the fringe of the Big City in the last decade. He is the grandchild or the great-grandchild of an immigrant. He has left behind the older parts of the city for the new and better life the suburbs seem to promise. He probably belongs to one of two general groups of people. He may be one of the "professionals"—the managers, the small businessmen, the college-trained technicians, the doctors, the lawyers, the labor leaders, the journalists who make up the new, upper-middle class. If he belongs to this group, he takes suburban living and all its comforts for granted. No matter what his parents or grandparents were, he feels that his education and position in society entitle him to a home of his own, a decent salary, and a large family.

If he belongs to the second group, his way of life may be no different from that of his neighbors in the first class, but his attitude is vastly different. For this group is made up of the white- and the blue-collar workers for whom the changes of the last twenty years have meant the possibility of a kind of life of which their predecessors would never have dreamed. In the past it was unusual for a factory worker or a clerk to own a new home of his own, but now it is becoming more and more common. For these people the move to Suburbia is not a matter of course but the beginning of a great adventure. They enter this adventure with hope but also with a lurking fear of another depression which would rudely shatter their dream.

The suburbanite may live in any one of several different kinds of communities. For Suburbia is by no means everywhere the same. The common thread which runs through all suburbs can be woven in many different fashions.

First of all, there is the "just getting started" suburb. Here is where newly-weds or those who are buying their first home make their start. The homes are simple, crowded, and relatively inexpensive; the people are young, the families are growing rapidly, and everything seems quite new. No one plans to spend his whole life in such a community. As soon as a bit more money turns up in the pay check, plans will be made for a move to a suburb where basements are better and houses are made of brick and have more than two bedrooms. At best such a neighborhood is not too stable; at worst it is a jungle of picture-windowed boxes on concrete slabs. These areas with their poor sewage, terrible streets, overcrowded schools, rising tax rates, wretched transportation, inadequate or nonexistent police and fire protection, and antique zoning ordinances have proved a gold mine to unscrupulous real estate operators and compliant public officials. They are the ready-made slums which are encroaching on the supposed pastoral bliss of the countryside.

Despite the hardships, there are advantages to living in such a suburb. Everyone is around the same age and in the same economic plight. There is a certain air of youthful romance and adventure about the community. Few of the inhabitants, however, are sorry to leave it when the big salary increase finally comes. The move to the better neighborhood is a sign of progress up the ladder to financial success. For a time, the suburbanite finds this new neighborhood quite a satisfactory place in which to live. The homes are bigger and better, public utilities are more reliable, people a bit older, teen-agers more numerous, and adults a little more staid. Since there is less thought of moving, there is more stability in the community. Lawns are well landscaped and trees are to be seen. Many of the neighbors, particularly the élite of the blue-collar workers who have managed to move into this suburb, show no signs of ever leaving. But, since the rising professional man realizes that he must have a home in keeping with his social status, there finally comes a day when he must move once again.

His third stop is in the "comfortable" suburb. Here he can choose his home from a wide variety of styles and enjoy well-manicured lawns creeping along a curving, tree-shaded street. His neighbors are quite a bit older. No one is under thirty and many are in their forties. Families are still large but older, and many of the children are planning weddings. The inhabitants are the professionals who have achieved a great deal of success but have not, in their own minds at least, become "rich." They are middle-rung executives, well-paid engineers, union business agents, successful small businessmen and insurance brokers.

They participate actively in community affairs and lead a busy, and at times frantic, social life—some of it centered on a country club. They are, however, more "outgoing" than their younger brothers and sisters who have yet to attain such affluence and security. There is likely to be a high rate of bleeding ulcers, heart attacks, and nervous breakdowns in this community. The strain of climbing the ladder has been too much for many psychic structures. This will be, however, the last stop on the suburbanite's climb to success. Along with most of his neighbors in the "comfortable" suburb, he has little intention of moving any more. The strain and effort necessary to attain a position which would make yet another move possible are thought to be too great. The suburbanite would rather stay where he is and enjoy life a little.

However, he may be unexpectedly fortunate, or he may put in the extra effort from force of habit, and end up in the "exclusive" suburb. Here are the fashionable homes of the "old families," the "new rich," and the top-bracket executives. If we have an aristocracy in this country, such a suburb is where it lives.

Wherever he lives and whatever his home is like, there is one thing that characterizes the life of the suburbanite—material abundance. It is prosperity that made the post-war suburbs possible, and it is the promise of further prosperity that keeps them going and furnishes the vision of an ever better life for the suburbanite. He lives surrounded by an unbelievable array of gadgets. Television, air conditioners, "hi-fi," power lawn mowers, deepfreezes, electric dishwashers, automatic dryers, automobiles, back-yard swimming pools, tranquillizing drugs, color transparencies—all vie for his attention. He takes these things for granted; they are a part of his heritage. He will admit to very little doubt that the future will offer him an even greater array of such marvelous gadgets. Purchasing all this material comfort means that he is living very close to or beyond his income. He is not able to save very much and may be deeply in debt. But he has faith in the ability of the American economy—or the American government—to see that these things are not taken from him.

Our nation has known prosperity before, but it has never enjoyed a prosperity which has affected so many people. The suburbanite with his income over $7,500, his large family, and his own home represents a profound social revolution. Even the poorest of the forty million suburbanites enjoys a standard of living which his grandparents (and perhaps his parents) would have thought belonged only to the well-to-do. Never before in the history of the human race has such a large portion of a people enjoyed the best in material comforts that its civilization had to offer.

Does such material abundance make him happy? It would be foolish to say that he does not enjoy the comforts or that he would give them up for peace of mind. Material possessions can never guarantee complete happiness, but they do make life somewhat more pleasant. A gadget-filled way of life may not be as satisfying as a suburbanite thought it would be when he began to collect worldly goods. Owning his own home may not bring the security and stability it seemed to promise. But few suburbanites are going to give up their gadgets or sell their homes. The physical ease and comforts which suburbanites take for granted are here to stay.

However, the pursuit of material abundance and the financial success which guarantees it creates psychological problems which the suburbanite's ancestors never had to face. Several penetrating observers of the American scene have detected a strange contradiction in our culture—one that can readily be observed within Suburbia. Margaret Mead points out that the American child is taught that he must observe a strict moral code and yet do all that is necessary for success in the business and professional world. David Riesman sees the change from the "inner-directed" man who is guided by the gyroscope of a built-in ethical code to the "other-directed" man whose main aim is to be skilled at the art of conforming to the various groups of which he is a part. William Whyte describes the transition from the "Protestant Ethic" to the Social Ethic of well-rounded, well-adjusted, well-balanced conformity. However we choose to describe these two motivational trends, the Suburban Man is caught up by both of them.

He is moving up, he wants to be a success; failure in his career is the worst thing that could happen to him. Study, hard work, diplomatic handling of his superiors—all these are indispensable during his arduous climb up the ladder toward financial success. The success compulsion is as strong as ever. Yet the suburbanite realizes, as his ancestors did not, that he must not give the appearance of striving too hard to be too successful too soon. He must strive for success with a certain nonchalance which indicates that he is still very much one of the crowd and would really hate to get ahead at the expense of his fellow men.

He must be career-centered. The house he lives in, the clothes he wears, the club he belongs to, the wife he marries—all these must be judged in terms of their effect on his career. If he is talented enough but his wife happens to have some odd habits like reading Plato, his company might even be able to send her to a special school where she can learn the gentle art of being a successful wife of a successful executive.

Personality tests strive to make his dedication to his career as private as the recreational life of a goldfish. He soon learns that the forty-hour week is for the wage slaves who have been smart enough to join unions and not for the rising young suburbanite. He quickly discovers that the sacrifices necessary to maintain his way of life make it almost impossible to enjoy all the advantages of such a life.

Hence he will protest about the insistent demands of the "rat race" and make it known that his family is far more important than his professional success. He tries not to think of what would happen to his family if professional success should be taken from him. His conscience bothers him about neglecting his home life, and so he does everything in his power to prove that his life is "family-centered." His friends in Suburbia are often parents of the friends his children have selected. He must put in the allotted number of hours with the Cub Scouts, the Pony League, the playground committee, and any other organization which promises to do something for his family. This is not hypocrisy. He loves his family and his community. He wants to be interested in them. He wants the happiness that comes from family life. He does hate the "rat race." Unfortunately, it is a bit difficult to be family-centered and career-centered at the same time.

The classic story about suburban life, *The Man in the Gray Flannel Suit,* expresses this dilemma perfectly. Its hero, Tom Rath, is given a chance at a job as president of a radio network. It will reduce his family life to a minimum but will give him great power, prestige, and influence. The other job he is offered would be considered much less "successful," but it will enable him to be a husband to his wife and a father to his children for more than a few hours a week. After considerable soul-searching, Rath chooses the lesser job, much to the joy of his wife, the novelist, the movie director, the Book of the Month Club, and Twentieth Century-Fox audiences. Most

young suburbanites claim they would make the same
choice. They do not want to be too "successful"—
just "comfortable." Unfortunately, few of them are
given an opportunity, as Rath was, to make a choice.
The problem torments them for most of their lives
without a solution ever being found.

This makes it difficult to attain another important
suburbanite goal—adjustment. In Suburbia, malad-
justment is almost as bad as failure. In fact, it is usually a mark of failure of one sort or another. The
race to be "outgoing" and well-adjusted is a feverish
one and is complicated by the fact that one must not
be over-adjusted or go out too much. Nothing can be
worse for a suburbanite matron than to hear that one
of her children is not doing well in social adjustment
at school. Good marks are no consolation if a youngster likes to associate with only a few children or even
at times just to play by himself. There is no room in
Suburbia for potential contemplatives.

Nevertheless, the suburbanite is often ridden by
anxiety and fear. He worries about his job, he worries about The Bomb, he worries about the stock
market, he worries about the property values, he worries about a depression, he worries about his ulcer, he
worries about his heart, he worries about his children
(especially the teen-age ones), he worries about inflation, and last of all he worries about his worries.
For, if he were well-adjusted, he would not worry,
and he knows he should be well-adjusted.

For all his material abundance, the suburbanite
finds something lacking in his life. Worldly success
does not seem to bring all that it should bring. Something seems to be missing. Occasionally the thought
will cross his mind that he might be wasting his time,
that he might be losing a chance for something far
more important than the things he has been seeking.
So far, however, he has not discovered what this other
thing might be.

It is very easy to damn the suburbanite way of life as "materialistic." But it seems that almost every other way of life that mankind has ever known has been "materialistic," too. Since man is part animal, it is natural enough that he will seek the things which bring comfort and convenience to the animal part of his nature. The suburbanite's problem is that an abundance of such comforts and conveniences has not brought him the tranquillity that he thought it would. Perhaps it is a distinct advantage. For perhaps the suburbanite will now begin to realize that he must look elsewhere and more profoundly for that form of Goodness in which our hearts must ultimately find rest.

II. The Church and the Suburbs

"Suburban domination may well be God's word of judgment on us as His Church. For our trespasses and complacency we have been delivered to Babylon."

DR. GIBSON WINTER, *The Christian Century, September 28, 1955*

The first part of this section is a study of the current religious revival, which is centered in the suburbs. Unless one understands the nature of this revival, the suburban religious phenomenon is inexplicable.

Next, the Catholic who has moved to the suburbs is compared to his parents and found, not wanting, but different.

The three concluding chapters describe some of the problems and adaptations of the Organized Church in a suburban environment.

4
The
Suburban
Revival[1]

One of the principal themes of Graham Greene's curious play *The Potting Shed* is the tragedy of an atheist who has lived to see his unbelief go out of fashion. The agnostic scientist is forced to live in a time when his dogmas are as passé as he thought the dogmas of orthodoxy were twenty years before. He has become as much an anachronism as he believed the fervent Christian to be a generation ago. In his usual somber fashion, Greene has touched on one of

[1] Seymour M. Lipset, in a recent issue of *The Columbia University Forum*, has questioned both the fact of the religious revival and the social service explanation frequently offered for the present religious enthusiasm. He claims that the alleged increase in church membership does not really represent a change in the religious attitudes of the population, but simply a change in the definition of what membership is. People who would not have been considered church members at the turn of the century are considered members today. Lipset attempts to demonstrate that there has been little change in the per cent of income contributed to churches, in the ratio of ministers to total population, and in church attendance.

However, he admits that there has been an increase in church attendance since the late forties. He also questions whether the social utility approach to religion is very new. There seems to be considerable evidence, he claims, that "Pealeism" is merely a modern form of a strain that has always been present in American religion (a claim that is backed up by the recent University of Chicago study, *Popular Religion*). Lipset seems to feel that America has existed in a state of continual religious revival and that the situation since 1945 is merely a slight upturn in something which has been a constant in our national culture. Whether this dissent from the Herberg theory will be accepted remains to be seen. It may serve, however, to put our present increase in religious interest in proper perspective.

the most significant events of our time. The forces
of organized religion, which several decades ago
seemed all but routed, are now in full command of
the field of battle and seem to be sweeping their foes
before them. Orthodoxy has refused to stay dead.
Despite the nearly fatal blows struck by Darwin,
Marx, and Freud, Christianity is once more current.
America seems to be in the midst of a great religious
revival in defiance of the predictions of all the experts
of years gone by.

Much ink has been spilled about the merits of this
"revival." It is exceedingly unfashionable in certain
circles to speak out in its defense. One can hardly
pick up a copy of a highbrow, or upper-middle brow,
journal and not find an article questioning or ridicul-
ing the "return to religion." An occasional voice for
the defense, like that of John Cogley or Father Walter
Ong, is quickly drowned out by the heavy-handed
satire of the skeptics. In the minds of most of the
liberal intelligentsia, the "revival" seems to have
become linked with witch-hunting, book-burning,
pseudo-moralism, and all sorts of other nasty things.
One writer goes so far as to say that the suburban variety of this "revival" is the Babylon to which Christianity has been delivered as a punishment for its sins.

There is reason to be skeptical of such broadside attacks. The "revival," like any other phenomenon in
contemporary American life, is an exceedingly complicated event, and one generalizes about it with considerable risk of oversimplification. It is not impossible that there might be more to the revival than its
critics would have us believe.

No one questions the increase in the quantity of
religious activity. In the quarter of a century between
1926 and 1950, the population of the United States
increased 28.6 per cent while membership in religious
bodies increased twice as rapidly. In the 1950's, population has been increasing at the rate of about 2 per

cent a year while religious membership is up about 3 per cent each year. Well over 60 per cent of our population now belongs to an organized religion—an increase of 300 per cent in 100 years and 200 per cent in 50 years. Not only has church membership gone up, but so has church attendance, if we are to judge by the many public opinion polls devoted to religion. Close to 500 million dollars is spent each year on new church buildings, and the total valuation of church property has increased by over 2.5 billion dollars in the last five yeears. Will Herberg, the foremost student of the "revival," reports that four new Catholic churches are opened every week.

Statistics cannot tell the whole story. There are many other signs on the American scene of the "return to religion." Politics, always a sensitive barometer of cultural change, furnishes some unmistakable evidence. A professed unbeliever would be anathema to either political party. It is a rare campaigner who does not mention God in each one of his talks. Some of the speeches of public officials sound almost like sermons. Church attendance is expected of men in high political office.

The mass media also reflects this new interest in things which can make some claim to being religious. It is hard to escape from religious songs on juke boxes, religious speakers on TV, religious articles in magazines, and religious movies in Cinemascope. The national taste has gone in for religion in a big way and religion has acquired an excellent market value.

Nor is the revival limited to the obviously popular levels. The intellectuals are once again more than a little interested in religion. Psychologists, sociologists, psychiatrists, and historians are all regarding religion wth new interest and respect. Kierkegaard, Maritain, Niebuhr, Buber, Tillich, Weil, and St. Thomas are names to be dropped if not authors to be read. In the words of H. Stuart Hughes, "Ten or fifteen years ago, no self-respecting 'enlightened' intellectual would have been caught dead with a religious interpretation of anything . . . now . . . the *avant-garde* is becoming old fashioned; religion is now the latest thing." [2]

The critics of the "revival" find little to criticize in the facts that are observable. Their quarrel is with what they consider the motives behind the new interest in religion. Religion, we are told, has become a social utility and people are religious because it is socially useful to be so. In a society which demands "adjustment" and "belonging" and "togetherness," religion is a necessary way to conform to the demands of the community. It has become an automatic and obvious social requirement. There are no atheists in the post-war suburban villages. Religion is necessary, to be a good parent; it is a strong bulwark for the American Way of Life, with which it has become practically identified. It helps one overcome feelings of inferiority and gives one poise and confidence in one's business and professional life. It brings a sense of personal dignity in a world where such dignity seems to be denied by massive forces beyond the control of the individual.

And so God becomes a "living doll," the "Man Upstairs," a "Great Helper" who underwrites free enterprise, prosperity, security, and the American Way of Life. Religion helps us to make friends, lose weight, and overcome the obstacles to rapid financial success. The thing that matters is not what one believes but that one believes. Dogma is not important, but going to the church of your choice on Sunday is enjoyable, thought-provoking, and a sure defense against communism. The Church becomes a vast social service organization and the clergy are expected to combine the skills of athletic directors and psychiatric counselors.

[2] Quoted in Will Herberg, *Protestant, Catholic and Jew* (New York: Doubleday, 1958).

This, the critics tell us, is the sheerest sort of idolatry. Religiousness has become the protection which David Riesman's "other directed man" has thrown up against the demands of true faith and authentic religion. God is no longer the real center of religious activity; man has usurped His place and twisted religion to his own ends. He has emptied it of all profound theological content and turned it into a cult of reassurance.

Thus speak the critics. One might wonder in passing about some of the men who are assuming the pose of defenders of the true faith. There might be some reason to suspect that a few of them are much more troubled by the revival's threat to agnosticism and secularism than by its corruption of ancient orthodoxy. On almost a priori grounds, these men would rule out the possibility of any kind of authentic religious revival; and that such a revival could take place among the suburban middle class is unthinkable. The Holy Ghost—if there is a Holy Ghost—could not possibly have such bad taste.

It is quite interesting to compare the attitude of a Catholic writer like *The Commonweal's* John Cogley with his secularist counterparts. Writers in, say, *The Nation* or *The New Republic,* with the (considerably attenuated) Reformation tradition of suspicion of the value of any human religious activity with reference to the Almighty, see nothing but hypocrisy and corruption in the "revival." Cogley, on the other hand, recognizing the Church's traditional ability to adapt itself to all sorts of concrete situations and to Christianize almost everything it encounters, sees the possibility that in the long run Westchester County might be a seed bed for future prophets.

Despite the fact that some of its proponents are in no position to defend traditional religion, the social utility explanation cannot be totally rejected. The careful study of the profoundly religious Jewish scholar Will Herberg shows that such an explanation contains a good deal of the truth.[3] It explains much of what passes for religion in our country in 1962. It accounts for a large amount of the new interest in religion. But it may be reasonably questioned if such a theory is anywhere near the full explanation. It might be wise to ask ourselves whether, alongside and intermingled with this sham revival, there is something which seems to reveal the Spirit of God blowing whither He will. For it is at least possible that the froth of religiosity may arise from an authentic spiritual ferment stimulated and sustained by Divine Grace.

The Catholic who wishes to investigate the revival as it affects his own Church would do well to begin by asking himself what other shape a true revival would take. How would it differ from the present phenomenon? Can we reasonably expect the middle-class American Catholic to don an Eric Gill smock, clutch a copy of Kierkegaard, and dash off to a remote, primitive farm? Some of the dissatisfaction with the revival comes from the fact that it is so very much a middle-class thing. But is this not the way any revival would manifest itself in such a middle-class country as the United States? The middle-class spirit of the revival would be reprehensible only if in the long run it failed to transcend itself. At present, however, it might be as natural as the troubadour spirit of the Franciscan revival or the military spirit of the Ignatian. Many of us might regret that the revival did not occur among the working class (whatever that might be in 1962), but this should not lead us to rule out the possibility that the Holy Spirit might work in the suburbs, too, or that His work in the suburbs might take on, initially at least, a distinctly suburban tinge.

The historian of the future might be forgiven if he

[3] *Op. cit.*

should judge, on the basis of the evidence available to him, that there was a strong and vital religious revival in the Catholic Church in the United States in the year 1962. He might not be much impressed by the statistics about church attendance or reception of the sacraments, since statistics by themselves tell nothing about fervor. He would admit, however, that twentieth-century American Catholics had reached a relatively high level of observable religious practice. But other information could not fail to impress him. The founding of eight Cistercian monasteries and one Carthusian (with a Camaldolese yet to come) in a decade would be a sure sign of great spiritual vigor. The five thousand delegates to the Liturgical Conference would prove that there was great interest in divine worship. The thousands who flocked to Notre Dame for Catholic Action conventions would convince our imaginary research scholar that the American lay apostolate was strong and healthy. Nor would he be able to overlook the massive school system, as much as he might puzzle over the controversy that raged around it.

If he could unearth a copy of *The New Cana Manual,* he would think that these twentieth-century Americans had great respect for the sacrament of matrimony. He would learn from a battered copy of the *Catholic Almanac* or the *Catholic Directory* the names of hundreds of Catholic organizations devoted to every sort of spiritual and temporal activity from scouting to metaphysics. He would be astonished at the amount of printed matter on Catholic subjects distributed during the 1950's and 1960's. He would not be able to overlook the many lay retreat movements, nor would he dare to underestimate the missionary efforts of American religious communities at home and abroad. He would even detect the faint beginnings of a limited-service lay mission movement which held great promise in the late years of this fascinating decade. The scholar of the future would find much that was wrong with the revival, but if he were told that it was all the result of the social utility of religion or the "joining" propensities of other-directed man, he would be more than slightly amused.

There is no reason to deny that there is a large element of Pealeism in the religious revival, Catholic or Protestant. Nor should there be unquestioning acceptance of all that passes for religion in our society. Let us grant that there is much love of material luxury, much narrow-mindedness and shallowness, much of what might well be called idolatry. Let us further admit that these things are bad—even horrible—and that all Christians must war against them. But let us not forget that grace builds on nature—even other-directed nature—and that the most noble religious movements in history have been tinged with natural elements which were not always the most admirable. The contemporary upswing in interest in religion may well provide a golden opportunity for the Mystical Body in the United States. If intelligent Catholics stand apart from it in disdain, they may run the risk of putting themselves in the same class as those fastidious Italian noblemen who wondered how any good could possibly come from the Poor Man of Assisi and his ragamuffin band of followers.

5
The
Catholic
Suburbanite

Fifteen years ago, it was fashionable to speak of the days of the "brick and mortar" priest as something of the dim and distant past. The period of great construction projects was thought to be over for the Church in the United States. A plateau had been reached. Today, however, many a suburban pastor, saddled with a small church, a big debt, a big school, and a bigger population, must longingly wish that the prophets had been right. A good part of the Catholic population is moving to the suburbs. Most Catholics are aware of the immense physical problems involved in the Church's keeping up with this migration. But few realize to what extent Suburbia represents a decisive turning point in the history of the American Church.

We have been, until recently, the Church of the working class. As late as 1946, 66 per cent of the Catholic population could be classed as members of the lower class (as opposed to less than 45 per cent for most Protestant groups in the same class). A generation ago, the vast majority of Catholics were either immigrants who had come in the last tidal wave of arrivals before World War I or the children of such immigrants. Common labor in the steel mills, stockyards, and construction gangs was the original occupation of the immigrant. Some of his children inched up the ladder and became policemen, firemen, workers in public utilities and transportation. A very few began to achieve success in law, medicine, and politics.

The situation is changing rapidly. Signs of the change could have been detected in the 1930's, but the Depression arrested its development. Since World War II, however, the educational benefits of the G. I. Bill, the social revolution of the '30's, and the booming Cold War prosperity have caused a profound modification in the fabric of American Catholic life. A great many Catholics are leaving behind their working-class and immigrant roots and becoming successful members of the rapidly expanding middle class. Tens of thousands of young Catholic college graduates have moved into the professions and are becoming an important part of the life of the nation. As a symbol and a summary of this great change, Catholics are moving to the suburbs.

The social and psychological problems arising from the extension of the Church into the suburbs are complex and frightening. There are those who would lament that our boast of being the Church of the poor and laboring is no longer totally accurate. (For that matter, the laboring—if they belong to a militant union—are not likely to be poor in this day and age.) Certainly we must make every attempt to keep a strong working-class base in our Church by trying to convert the new, and largely non-white, lower class. But we must also face the deep and tangled problems that many Catholics are encountering as they become suburbanites.

First of all, there is the problem of the material prosperity of Suburbia. The Church, of course, has never condemned as such the possession of the goods of this world. On the contrary, she has affirmed that a certain moderate comfort is a distinct help to salvation. Nor has the Church opposed the improvements of the age of technology. The Church is not against the machine, atomic energy, or automation. But the problem for the Catholic suburbanite is more subtle. Our national prosperity is based on a constantly expanding economy. Last year may have been a good year, but if this year is not better than last it will be a bad year. The sale of four million automobiles would have been staggeringly good several years ago. This year it would mean a severe depression. If our economy is to remain healthy, it must constantly produce and sell more goods.

If more goods are to be bought, however, more people must feel they need them. So our economy is geared to constantly expanding human needs; and our advertising is fashioned to create these needs. Yesterday's luxuries become today's necessities. What is an interesting novelty today will be a part of the American way of life tomorrow. A car whose design was "years ahead of its time" two years ago is now, from the fashion point of view, obsolete. If the nation is to continue prosperous, its people must want more, more, more.

Such an economic situation may not be in itself an evil. But we have no experience in the ways of harmonizing an expanding-need culture with the traditional teachings of Christian frugality, with the spirit of poverty. It may be possible to want more, more, more and still not lay up treasures in this world where the moth consumes and rust destroys. It may be possible to give no overanxious heed to what we should eat, or what we should drink, or what we should put on when the mass media proclaim in full color that they can array us with greater glory and equip us with greater power than was Solomon's. It may be possible to sit in an air-conditioned ranch-house and watch a color-television set and still not be attached to the things of this world. It may, in short, be possible to harmonize the world of the gadget and the world of the spirit. All these things are possible, but they are not easy.

The Catholic suburbanite is not a crass materialist. He does not pile up possessions for mere love of wealth. He is extremely generous to all sorts of charitable endeavors. He will spare no expense to provide a Catholic education for his large and growing family. He is, in all likelihood, more fervent in his religious duties than were his parents. He is probably an active parishioner and by his own lights an excellent Christian. In fact, he and his fellows have, it would seem, reached a level of *observable religious practice* seldom, if ever, surpassed by a large group of people in the history of the Church.

But the problem of reconciling the gadget and the spirit remains to be solved. In fact, the suburbanite Catholic is hardly aware that the problem exists. So he looks around at his great material wealth (and great it is, by almost any standards that mankind ever knew) and wonders whether his dream house is not getting small, whether he should not get a station wagon with push-button transmission, whether he should not perhaps air-condition the whole house, and whether it's not time to get a power lawn mower or join the local country club. It does not occur to him that such anxieties might interfere with his seeking first the Kingdom of God and His justice.

With prosperity and abundance there comes a second problem for the suburban Catholic. He is a successful, educated, and independent man. True enough, his future may be at the mercy of all sorts of forces out of his control; but he prides himself on the fact that he is a free American and makes his own decisions. His faith is real, but it is by no means the legendary simple faith of the Breton fisherman or the somewhat less simple faith of his immigrant grandmother. He has been taught to question things and to ask why. His priests are no longer the only educated, or even necessarily the best-educated, men in the community. There are a number of people who are capable of assuming the traditional place of the pastor as the single social leader of the neighborhood.

The suburbanite feels free to disagree with his clergy on certain procedural matters and to do so forcefully and persistently.

This is not to say that he is anticlerical, but only that the social relationship between the clergy and the laity is changing as an inevitable result of the changing social structure of the world the American Catholic lives in. As one priest sociologist has observed, from the social viewpoint the pastor can no longer afford to be the unquestioned ruler, but now must, if he wishes to be effective, play the role of a quarterback who calls the signals and then co-operates with the rest of the team in the execution of the play.

This subtle change in the accidental structure of the clergy-laity relationship is merely a manifestation of a deeper problem Catholic Suburbia poses. The suburbanite, for all his conformity to the demands of the social groups to which he belongs, is more than a little skeptical of naked authority. "The Church says so" has ceased to be an all-powerful argument. As Father John Thomas has pointed out, the rational foundations of faith and the logical connections between dogmatic beliefs and specific moral imperatives must be made crystal-clear if American Catholics are to be convinced.[1] If an executive of a large corporation cannot be treated in the same fashion as his grandfather, it would follow that something more than the Baltimore Catechism is required for a graduate of a college and professional school.

No one would claim that, absolutely speaking, such changes have to be made; the word of the Church on dogma and discipline is still final. But in the area of sound psychology and effective administration, gradual changes seem inevitable. Authority will not be diminished. It will merely be used in a different way in different times. Progress in this area of the tension

[1] *American Catholic Family* (New York: Prentice-Hall, 1956).

between authority and independence is being made, rapidly. Both the clergy and their suburbanite congregations seem patient and eager to learn. But only an incurable optimist would believe that some frictions are not bound to occur as a new relationship between priest and people grows in the suburbs.

A third difficulty facing the Church in the suburbs may be, in the long run, the most perplexing. For in the suburb the Catholic is regarded, at last, as a full-fledged American. The ghetto walls are crumbling The old national parishes are breaking up. The Catholic suburbanite rides the same commuter train, wears the same brand of suit, reads the same paper, and does the same kind of work as does his non-Catholic neighbor. He may not be completely accepted by Protestants; but he is well on his way. Thirty years ago most non-Catholics were horrified at the thought of Al Smith as President; today many were willing to vote for John F. Kennedy. Suburbia, with its conglomeration of nationalities and religions, seems the ultimate melting pot. In the externals of life there is little to distinguish the Catholic suburbanite from his Protestant neighbor. Even such old criteria as large families or regular Sunday attendance at church have ceased to be significant.

This Americanization of the immigrant groups is a good thing; but is not an unmixed blessing. Catholics can accept much of the American way of life with little hesitation; but in certain matters—birth control, divorce, and premarital sex experience, for example—we must part company with many Americans. In national parishes and the old neighborhoods, Catholics were somewhat insulated from the infection of pagan influences. In the suburbs they are in the main line of the enemy's fire. This is not to argue that we should retreat into our ghetto. We could not if we wanted to. But the fact must be faced that the suburban Catholic could become *too* American. There is some danger that he will begin to share the common American notion that one religion is practically as good as another. When this happens, he has ceased to be much of a Catholic, no matter how American he may be.

The problems are complex and serious. There are no simple solutions. If the problems are great, however, so also are the opportunities. The Catholic with his doctrine of the Mystical Body may well be able to develop in the suburbs a spirituality which will end the secularism separating the world of the spirit from the world of the gadget. The educated, independent, suburbanite parishioner could become a zealous, dedicated lay apostle bearing witness to the Word of God in areas the priest could never reach.

It is too early to predict the exact shape suburban Catholicism will take. Its techniques and methods are still new and vague. They are being worked out by the system of trial and error, but the final product may well be considerably different from the Catholicism we were used to ten years ago. New things are beginning to stir in the American Church; and we do not know where they will end. The Liturgical Movement, the Catholic Action organizations, Adult Education programs—all hold great promise.

From the point of view of suburban problems, among the most interesting and typical of the "new things" are the Christian Family Movement and other movements with similar techniques and goals, such as Cana Family Action. Although C. F. M. is not a specifically suburban organization and in some areas has considerable strength outside the suburbs, it still seems fair to say that in most dioceses the backbone of the movement is largely suburban. Its phenomenal growth in the last decade has been parallel to the expansion of Suburbia, and its techniques are particularly agreeable to the suburban mentality. It also suffers to some extent from the limitations of the suburban vision. For these reasons, this movement may repay a few minutes' examination.

The appeal of C. F. M. to the new middle class on the edge of the city is obvious enough. Its main concerns—home, family, neighborhood, local community —are the main concerns of the suburban man and his wife. Its technique—group discussion—is a process with which the suburbanite is familiar from his work life. Its attention to the strains of the husband-wife and parent-child relationships meets a deeply felt suburban need. Its attempt to bring religion into closer contact with daily life fits in perfectly with the current revival of interest in religion, which is particularly strong in the suburbs. Its avowed goal, "For Happier Families," is one which no suburbanite would dream of questioning. In short, C. F. M. has been a "natural." Its founders probably never dreamed it would spread with such fantastic speed. Yet, when one looks back on its first decade, one can see it was the right organization in the right place at the right time.

C. F. M. is by no means perfect. It has had its mistakes, its hesitations, its gropings. At times it has tended to get bogged down in procedural swamps. It is not, and never will be, more than a limited, partial answer to the problems the Church faces in Suburbia. But within its limitations C. F. M., along with its sister family organization, the Cana Movement, has offered some tentative suggestions that the suburban Church can ill afford to ignore.

Its persistent study of Holy Scripture has brought out clearly the tension between material abundance and an other-worldly kingdom. It has evolved a relationship between priest and membership which both clergy and laity have found fruitful. Its formation through action has given the Church a pool of intensely dedicated lay people capable of doing great things. Finally, it has helped members to grasp the relationship between belief and daily moral practice and hence equipped them to influence the secular world with little fear of being corrupted by it.

C. F. M. still has many problems to face. It is difficult for the suburbanite to enlarge his social consciousness beyond home, family, and neighborhood to the work group, the city, the nation, and the world community. The strongest criticism of the movement, however, is self-criticism; and it seems fair to guess that C. F. M.'s contribution to the suburban Church is far from over.

There is a considerable amount of controversy as to whether, in the long run, the suburban migration is a good thing for the Church. Such controversy seems pointless. As in all social changes, there are elements of good and bad mixed in a tangled skein. Whether the net result will show the good outbalancing the bad can be determined only by the historians of the future; but what the net result will be depends, under God, on the free will of men. If one tries to survey Catholic Suburbia with some objectivity, one can find many reasons for a cautious hope.

6
The
Suburban
Parish[1]

It was not too many years ago that American Catholics were being warned that the decline of the national parish would have dire results for the Church. Social scientists visiting from Europe had deduced, not without reason, that the national parishes were the main explanation of the fact that the American Church had not lost the urban working class. Therefore, as the national parishes broke up and the third generation of immigrants became thoroughly Americanized, there would be an inevitable tendency to drift away from the Church, since the Church in its national-parish manifestation would be part of the Old World culture which the new Americans would reject.

It was a fine theory, but like so many fine theories it was simply not true. The European theorists made the mistake of assuming that the drift away from the Old World religion, which indeed was characteristic of the second generation, would continue in the third. As the studies of Herberg and Hansen have shown, the tendency of the third generation is rather to drift back into religious practice as it seeks some sort of

1 Perhaps it should be noted in passing that this discussion concerns the parish as a natural community or quasi-community. The parish is also a supernatural community, with functions of worship, sanctification and religious education; these supernatural functions can go on even when the natural community is almost non-existent. Nevertheless, grace builds upon nature and to some extent the effectiveness of the supernatural operations depends in God's ordinary providence on the solidarity of the natural. Hence man is more likely to go to church if his pastor knows him by name.

social identity.[2] We have no reliable statistics on the extent of this return to religion in the suburbs, but few question the fact that some sort of counter drift is going on. With certain national groups such as the Irish there is no question of a counter drift, since there was little drift away in the first place. We hear considerably less today about the problem of "leakage" from the Church than we did a decade ago. This is no proof that leakage is not as serious a problem as it was in the past; but it would seem that the social trends of the post-war world have not made it a noticeably more serious problem. Quite the contrary; the suburban religious revival may have made it somewhat less serious.

If one is to seek a reason for the failure of the prophecies about the decline of religious practice, one might find ·that the European scholars and their American admirers put too much emphasis on the fact that the modern urban parish is not a community. It is not a community in the sense that the small, stable, integrated rural parishes in European peasant culture were communities. But this type of community is a vanishing thing in modern civilization. The national parish certainly did not approximate it. On the natural level people identified with the national parish because it met certain social needs which they felt. The transitional parish, one might call it "second generation" parish, met certain other needs. The suburban parish is no exception: if it is to provide a natural community, it must meet still other needs.

The hypothesis might be hazarded that the American parish has always been a social service organization and that in different circumstances the type of service offered has been different. The "national" parishes attempted to meet the problems of the new immigrants; in the new suburban neighborhood the parish

2 Cf. *Protestant, Catholic, Jew,* passim.

is trying to meet the problems of the third generation. The transition from Old Neighborhood to suburb then is not a transition from religious practice to non-practice, but rather from one type of social service to another. On the whole, the transition is not being made too badly.

It is still too early in the history of the suburban parish to say what new forms will ultimately be evolved or how different these forms will be from the old ones. Again, there is no such thing as a typical suburban parish because there is no typical suburb or typical pastor. Nevertheless, it is possible to detect some general outlines of development which give interesting hints to the future.

First of all, the suburban pastor is a pioneer with an extremely difficult physical task. The construction of the American parish plant follows a rather definite pattern—a school with a hall which can be used for Mass, a convent, rectory, church, and perhaps a social center with school addition. While the construction of such a plant has never been particularly leisurely, it was not unusual for it to be spread over a twenty-year period. In the suburbs it seems imperative that it be done within five years, or ten at the very most. Growth and expansion in the community goes on at a frantic pace, and the parish is expected to keep up. Hence the suburban pastor normally finds himself burdened with a huge debt and facilities that are rapidly becoming inadequate. It is not at all rare for a new school to be too small even before it is finished. To complicate his problem the pastor is faced with parishioners who are only too quick to complain that he is (a) demanding too much money and (b) seems reluctant to provide more classrooms and (c) is holding back the parish which will never amount to anything until the pastor stops worrying about finances and gets some more activities going. Or provides space for the Cub pack to meet. Or builds a new parking lot.

The worry about finances, however, is not unwarranted, especially in the early days of a parish. Virtually all the members of a new parish are mortgaged to the hilt; they are paying high taxes for poor public service and an expensive public school system. They may be as generous as they possibly can and yet have very little money to contribute to their parish. More than one parish has two thousand children of grammar school age and literally no money to build a school. Some pastors never escape the problem, since their parishes are the "ready-made slums" where only the poorest of the suburbanites will live. Once families make a little more money, they will move to a better suburb. These parishes with hundreds of couples in their twenties or early thirties and three hundred baptisms a year may be lively, but they will never be stable, and their pastor's life expectancy cannot be too great.

These are the construction problems of the suburban parish at its best. This is the picture in dioceses which have the resources and personnel to stay not too far behind the pace of suburban expansion. The situation is much grimmer where the Catholics are a limited minority of the population and the suburban pastor must add size and distance to his other difficulties. In some areas of the country, there simply are no religious facilities for the Catholic suburbanite. The Church in these areas is faced with problems as grave as any it has faced in its history in the United States.[3]

[3] Exactly what the suburban expansion can mean to the Church is shown in that most suburban of all dioceses, Los Angeles. According to John E. Truxaw in *Ave Maria* (May 23, 1959), 70 new parishes and 138 new parochial schools have been opened in Los Angeles in the past 11 years. The diocese has expanded from 690,000 to 1,243,500 in the past decade, and newcomers are arriving at the rate of more than 55,000 a year (more than the entire population of some 20 American dioceses). More than 1,000 lay teachers assist the 2,100 religious in the Catholic schools, and

This pioneer situation is bound to influence the tone of a suburban parish. The never-ending financial crisis will inevitably affect the course of development. In a few places radical innovations have been made in which the laity have been assigned all sorts of functions that the clergy formerly reserved to themselves—for example, book-keeping, census work, planning, fund raising. Two reasons are given for these experiments: the priest just cannot perform all of these functions, and if the laity do them, they may begin to appreciate the problems of their priests. In other parishes, teacher aids and home religion classes are helping to alleviate the shortage of classrooms and teachers. Whether any of these innovations will become widespread remains to be seen. Not a few priests are beginning to suspect that even more radical changes will be necessary if the suburban parish is to keep up with the growth around it.

Financial crisis need not be a complete liability. A diplomatic and patient priest can use it as a means of welding a solidarity that is matchless on the natural level. The spirit generated by professionally planned fund drives proves that it is not impossible to build a sense of community through the common overcoming of grave obstacles.

A second characteristic of the suburban parish is that, like the suburb of which it is a part, it is child-centered. It is very much to be feared that the Cath-

even though the number of enrollments in Catholic schools has trebled in ten years (about 150,000), Truxaw estimates that there are still some 200,000 Catholic children in public schools. To complicate the problem there were only 8,143 Catholic deaths in the area as opposed to 52,845 infant baptisms. Despite the tremendous efforts of the clergy and laity of the diocese, many, many years will be necessary before the effects of the suburban boom on the Church are brought under control. In this way, as in so many others, Los Angeles, may well point the way to complications of the future. What happens there today will happen in ten other dioceses within a very few years.

olic suburbanite thinks of his parish primarily as a place for his children. Here they are to be educated—not just in religion, but in all the social graces, dancing included. Here they are to receive their instructions about sex. Here they are to have their recreation and their athletic programs. Here they can be sent to get them out of their mother's hair for five hours each day. Here is where the blame is to be assigned if they act up or do not get good grades. Here is the place for a good part of their social life when they become teen-agers.

Of course, the school has always been an important element of the American parish, but one doubts that it has been quite the center of parish life that it has become in the suburbs. Even the children themselves think of it in this fashion, and they will use the parish name by itself when they are referring to their school or its recreation yard. When they leave the grammar school to go to high school they think of themselves less as parishioners than they did before; and the collegian considers himself to be, for all practical purposes, no longer a member of the parish. He feels that he will become a parishioner once again when he moves to another parish and begins to raise a family of his own.

Activities dealing with children and their problems are the most popular in the parish. Home School Conferences (the Catholic version of the PTA) attract men whom the priests barely see from one end of the year to the other. A Sunday afternoon football game will have a larger crowd than a Forty Hours procession. Couples can be sold on Cub Scout work who wouldn't touch CFM with a ten-foot pole. A lecture on problems of education will draw twice as many people as one on any other topic. Eighth grade social life will stir up almost as much controversy as the suspicion that a member of an "undesirable" minority group is about to move into the community.

Such interest in children is of course commendable, but there is some danger that suburbanites are beginning to think of the parish as a glorified day-nursery and the priests and nuns as highly trained baby sitters.

Child-centered activities, however, are not the only social services a parish offers or is expected to offer. A "bad" parish is one where there is "nothing going on," and a "good" parish is one where there is a never-ending bustle of activities—bowling leagues, discussion groups, Catholic Action organizations, library committees, pamphlet rack committees and just about any other possible kind of organization, committee, or meeting that the mind of man can conceive. By no means all parishioners or even a majority are involved in such activity, but a good many of them are, and one gets the impression that a far higher percentage are active than in the typical older parish.

The question of the priest's relation to these activities will be discussed in the next chapter; however, it does seem quite clear that all the organizations and projects of a suburban parish do tend to promote some sort of loyalty and some sort of identification. The exact nature of this loyalty and its religious value is not easy to determine in our present state of knowledge. Most suburbanites, lay and clerical alike, would think that the presumption was in favor of the value of the activities until the contrary was proved.

Suburbanites demand an extremely high degree of competence from their clergy. In fact, at times they seem to demand almost the impossible. A priest must be a good preacher, a skilled counselor, a lively socializer, a gifted organizer, an accomplished diplomat, a shrewd coach or athletic director, a wise planner and builder and a genius with teen-agers. He must be as skillful in his many diverse areas of operation as the up-and-coming suburbanite professional is expected to be in his own area. Even minor failures and mistakes are often treated with a savage criticism which is strangely unrealistic. At times one begins to wonder if the suburbanite does not secretly resent his clergy. Could it be that the suburbanite who has had to struggle for every bit of status and prestige he has resents men who have prestige and status ex officio? Could it be that a man who must worry constantly about security for himself and his family resents the comfort and security the clergy possess without any necessary competence? Could it be that a man who dares not make a major mistake lest it ruin his career resents a man whose career is not seriously threatened by any number of seeming blunders? Perhaps not; but there is at least a possibility that in the suburbs can be found the beginning of a sentiment which, while not anticlericalism in the European sense, can nevertheless pose a fairly serious problem for the future, a problem which can be solved only with great patience and honesty on both sides.

At least one serious religious difficulty comes from the very fact that a parish is in the suburbs; like the suburb it tends to become isolated from many aspects of life. In a steel-mill parish the economic problems of the day are self-evident. In a racially changing neighborhood, the problems of the migrant groups are obvious. In a slum neighborhood, the implications of metropolitan development are not to be denied. In a university parish the intellectual currents of the age cannot very well be ignored. But the ordinary suburban parish is so concerned with its own problems of growth and so busy building up its own tight little community that it is not the best platform for social action in the world of human activities and ideas. For the husbands and fathers this is particularly true. They spend so few of their waking hours within the parish boundaries that they are apt to think of the parish as a place for their women and children, with little to contribute to the important decisions of life. No one has yet discovered an effective way of linking the suburban parish with the larger economic and social questions of the day.

The suburban parish looks quite different from its predecessors. Its functional church, low-slung school, and the acres of parking space represent a new image on the American scene. Its method of operation seems to be undergoing change from the techniques of the Old Neighborhood. Its human relational problems are new and more complicated. It has a reservoir of past experience to draw from, but it must provide new solutions of its own if it is to fulfill its purpose. Despite all the changes, however, it still must be a place where God is worshiped; a place where His Gospel is preached. If these basic tasks are not its ultimate goal, then, however successful it may appear to be on the natural level, its sound and fury are nothing more than the clash of cymbals.

7

The
Suburban
Priest

"Going My Way," the almost legendary Bing
Crosby-Barry Fitzgerald Academy Award winner of
the middle '40's, has recently enjoyed a second spring
of popularity on the TV networks — complete with
full-page advertisements in the *New York Times*. One
cannot hear the catchy melody of "Swinging on a
Star" without remembering the minor controversy
that raged in Catholic journals twelve years ago about
Hollywood's most famous version of clerical life. To
defenders of "Going My Way" this "humanization"
of the priest was a major propaganda victory for the
Church; to the critics of the movie, the piano-pound-
ing, golf-playing clergyman was a dangerous distortion of the sacramental role of the priesthood.[1]

For the purposes of this chapter the controversy
need not be resolved; but the renewed popularity of
"Going My Way" does prompt us to ask a most interesting question: What is the image of the priesthood
in the minds of most American Catholics? Virtually
everyone who saw "Going My Way" would have admitted if asked that the main task of the priest was to
say Mass and give absolution for sins; so would Catholics today. But one wonders if this theoretical knowledge has much practical relevance. One is tempted
to believe that the common operational image of the
priesthood is that of a social welfare resource person.

In the present state of religious sociology this cannot be proved with scientific exactness. One must rely
on general impressions, little hints, and partially

[1] And now the TV series based on "Going My Way" promises
to be the "Ben Casey" of the current season.

founded suspicions. Nevertheless, there is at least some reason to think that the Catholic layman views his pastor primarily as an administrator of a large plant and the superintendent of an educational institution. The curate is looked upon as a part-time recreational supervisor and a part-time bargain-basement psychiatric counselor. The church is judged as a social service center. A pastor may be criticized if his school is too small, or outmoded, but he is rarely criticized for not quickening in his people a realization of the vital role of the liturgy. A curate may be condemned for not showing up at all of the grammar school football games or not preventing a fight at his prep club, but rarely is any complaint registered if he is not too attentive to his apostolic formation groups.

William Whyte in his study of the suburbs points out how many Catholics criticize their parishes for not furnishing the same kind of center for busy activities as do the non-dogmatic United Protestant Churches. The criticism is typical; most Americans expect their clergy to be what the chaplains are expected to be in the armed services—morale officers. Insofar as Catholics share this view, they are assimilating an attitude alien to their own tradition.

Underlying the question of what the people expect of their priests in the way of social services, there is a deeper problem: What is the role of the priest in the twentieth century? At all times in the history of the Church, the priest's job has been to sanctify, rule, and teach. But, as circumstances change, the precise way these roles are exercised can undergo considerable transformation. One cannot imagine St. Augustine at a basketball game, St. Jerome as a non-directive counselor, or St. John Vianney at a high school social. This is not to say that the old approaches were necessarily better than the ones we are using now, but it is to say that the external circumstances of priestly work can vary tremendously from one era to another.

The precise difficulty seems to be that at present we are living during a time of transition from one era to another. For many centuries the parish priest was the unquestioned social and intellectual leader of his flock, whether it was in a European village or an American national parish. The ideal pastor was kindly and paternal, but still very much the one who made decisions. There was no need for him to accommodate himself to the special demands of his people because normally there were no special demands. His role was never subject to the slightest doubt. He may not have been liked, his policies may not have been popular, but no one would have thought of suggesting that he should change his function in the community.

Whatever its merits, this situation is rapidly becoming a thing of the past. Some pastors may still be the dominant figures in their neighborhoods, but it is only a man of exceptional skill and personality who can play this role in the new suburban parishes. Nor, as we have said, are the clergy the only educated people in a community, or even necessarily the best-educated. The people are no longer as much impressed by their priest's learning as they are by his competence at what they take to be his functions.

Hence it would seem that the image of the priest as a social and intellectual leader is gradually changing into that of a resource person in construction, education, psychiatry and recreation. The Bing Crosby priest of "Going My Way" seems to be the successor to the Barry Fitzgerald of the old-fashioned way. This might not necessarily be a bad thing; it certainly seems to be what the people demand of their clergy. But it would perhaps be wise to ask some questions about this trend while it is developing.

First of all, to what extent are we aware of the fact that our Protestant brothers are doing the same thing and in many cases doing it better? Most priests, one would imagine, were vastly amused with *Time's* account a few years ago of the "beaver-busy" Protestant community church with its daily round of "dances, pageants, picnics, buzz sessions, casserole brigades, fishing groups, hot-rod clubs, camps for all ages, and ten choirs." Yet are there not many Catholic parishes in which a tremendous amount of energy is absorbed in the same round? And how many of the priests who smiled at the picture of the young Methodist minister surrounded by teen-agers on a bus bound for Lake Geneva have not been in a similar situation many times in their pastoral lives? In attempting the same type of program, is there a danger that our spiritual resources will be overlooked in the shuffle? Perhaps not, but at least this is a question which we must ask ourselves.

Secondly, if we are to grant that the parish is to be also a social welfare center, to what extent could many of the activities be handled by laymen? Coaching a football team might under certain circumstances be one of the most apostolic works of a priest; in other conditions it might furnish a priest with needed relaxation; but in yet other situations there seems little reason why the laity should not have most of the responsibility for a parish athletic program. The grace of Orders does not qualify a priest to be an athletic director, and teen-age recreational activity is not the primary responsibility of the clergy. If parents want this type of organization badly enough, there is little excuse for their not supervising it themselves and bearing some of the responsibility for the success or failure of a parish teen-age program.

Even in the area of counseling several questions might be asked. No one could see any objection to the clergy's knowing as much as possible about psychology. Yet is it the function of a priest to be a full-time psychiatric counselor, as so many Protestant ministers are? Spiritual guidance is one thing and psychotherapy is something quite different. We need, it would seem, far more priests trained in counseling than we have; but is this in the nature of things, or is it simply that there is a lack of Catholic laymen who are psychologists? Is it not possible that in the ideal order of a priest's job would be to give spiritual guidance, and to know enough psychology to turn neurotics and incipient psychotics over to trained laymen? At present the priest is often forced to play the role of psychologist because there are not enough psychologists, or because the fees for treatment are too high, or because many people feel that there is a social stigma attached to consulting a psychiatrist.

Thirdly, we might ask how effective in the long run our social service activities really are. Presumably we engaged in these activities because they are a help in saving souls. Perhaps they are; but is their effectiveness commensurate with the time, energy and effort put into them? Is it not possible that a priest's time could be budgeted in more economical fashion? It may be that social service functions are the best preparation for preaching and sanctifying that we have at our disposal; but let us not merely take this for granted.

I am myself responsible for an athletic program, have shepherded teen-agers on countless picnics, and have even tried, though not too successfully, to use the non-directive counseling technique. Like most of my fellow priests I have enjoyed these activities and will continue to work at them. I have no idea what an alternative would be. There is no reason why liturgy and Catholic Action cannot exist along with social service or why there cannot be a close connection between the essential and peripheral functions of a priest. But I am simply not sure that the present complex of clerical activities is completely suited to the needs of the Church and its members in the second half of the twentieth century. The question as to the form the priestly role should take in our age is still very much open.

One question might be asked of the liturgical movement. Is there any way in which the liturgical movement can profit from the social welfare approach? This does not mean that we would put the liturgy at the service of social service, but rather the opposite. Liturgists have been tempted on occasion to object strongly to social service activities as a waste of priestly time. It is to be hoped that a sufficient number of disavowals of such an attitude have been made in this book to prevent the writer's being accused of holding the same position. Yet the demand for such services seems to be so great and the clerical response to the demand so enthusiastic that the entire social service concept cannot be rejected out of hand. It is possible that social service can be a means of building the natural community that a parish needs to be before it can become a conscious supernatural community at worship. Perhaps the liturgical movement could devote more consideration in the future to the parish as a natural community.

8

The Parish as a Community

Much ink has been spilled in recent years on the state of the urban parish as a community. There has been general agreement that most urban parishes are not communities, but mere collections of people with few or no bonds to the parish or their fellow Catholics. The urban parish is but a segment of David Riesman's lonely crowd. Much anguish has been generated through comparisons between the anonymous apartment house parish and the Christian community which existed in peasant society. Considerable heat has arisen over the question as to whether the parish, since it is no longer a community, ought to be abandoned in favor of some other form of apostolate.

Perhaps it is time to question some of the assumptions which have been at the root of the discussion. For one of the key assumptions has been the theory of mass society which has become less and less respectable in sociological circles during the last two decades and, in the form assumed in the parish discussion, is held by practically no one.

One must realize that the men who shaped modern sociology were concerned above all else with one phenomenon. Men of the late nineteenth and early twentieth century that they were, they saw traditional agrarian, peasant society being replaced by modern urban industrialism. Much of their work was an attempt to explain or at least describe this change. Tönnies spoke of *Gemeinschaft* (communal society) versus *Gesellschaft* (contractual society). Weber spoke of traditional and legal (or bureaucratic) society. Durkheim described segmental and organic societies. In this country Charles Horton Cooley developed the notion of the "primary group" based on intimate, diffuse, face-to-face contact.

What was common to all the writers was the notion that in the change from agrarianism to industrialism, human relations bonds were being destroyed. Man was no longer enmeshed in a net of tightly knit personal ties. There were very few goups intevening between the family and the great society. The intimate, satisfying ties of the primary group were vanishing from human life. Instead of being involved in warm personal relations with his neighbor, his pastor, the other members of his village, his relatives beyond the nuclear family, the urban citizen was now spending his life in a series of formal, highly impersonal relations, of which the classic in all the textbooks seems to be the relationship between the bus driver and the man who rides the bus.

For several decades, then, the contrast was between communal, primary group societies and contractual, "secondary" group societies. One got the impression that, with the exception of family ties—and even these were getting weaker—there was no *Gemeinschaft* left in urban industrialism. Society was composed of a mass of anonymous, rootless individuals, with little in the way of intimate ties to their fellow men. Community had vanished, there was only the lonely crowd.

Theorists of the Catholic parish were quick to apply this theory to the urban parish, pointing out how large it was, how infrequent contacts were between the pastor and his flock, how little sense of belonging the people felt, how it differed from the tight, intimate community of the peasant village. French theorists became almost mystical about the lack of community in the urban parish, and a fair number of Americans did not hesitate to agree completely, even though, if they had but looked out their windows, the phenomenon of the national parish should have at least caused them to ask some questions.

In recent years the theory of mass society has come under heavy attack. The prelude to the attack was the work of Elton Mayo and his colleagues, who discovered the informal work group in the industrial plant and learned that it was this group—small, intimate and face-to-face (and hence impossible according to the mass society theory)—that actually determined the level of output of its members. The most devastating attack, however, came from a young Harvard Fellow named William F. Whyte who went into the slums of South Boston in the late thirties to study the social disorganization which everyone said would be there. Much to his surprise he found, not disorganization, but a high degree of organization. The Norton Street Gang which shaped the lives of its members was but a small unit in a complex system of social controls by which the Italian Community of South Boston held itself together. *Gemeinschaft* was apparently still very much alive in *Gesellschaft* society.

The assaults on the mass society theory now began in earnest. Various research projects on the flow of influence demonstrated conclusively that influence tended to flow in two steps—from the mass media to a group of friends or work associates, and then from the group to its members. Thus the famous Decatur study showed that women made their fashion, marketing, and entertainment decisions not as isolated members of a mass society but rather as members of a small group under the influence of whoever was the "opinion specialist" in the group. The various studies of voting patterns demonstrated the tremendous influence of small group membership on voting decisions. Studies of the various armies—Russian, German, American—during the second World War proved that the small primary group (the squad) was the backbone of the army and that soldiers fought because of loyalty to this group more than for any other reason. Indeed, in the Wehrmacht it was the collapse of the small group which had been held together by the authority of non-coms which signaled the end. Anthropologists are even beginning to say that the extended family is by no means as irrelevant in modern society as had previously been thought.

Similar findings have come out of the study of religious membership. Will Herberg suggested that a religious group was not merely a contractual association which covered certain aspects of a person's life but a real community, a kind of super ethnic group which gave its members "social location" between the family and the larger society. Gerhard Lenski has recently offered data to confirm Herberg's theory and to show that the religious community to which one belongs influences every aspect of one's value system. Studies of suburban congregations—Catholic and non-Catholic alike—have shown that the churches on the fringes of the city are beehives of community activities.

As a result of these—and numerous other—findings, modern sociologists are trying to avoid the distinction between community and mass societies, between primary group societies and secondary group societies. What they are more interested in today is primary group experience; they take it as proved that even in a society marked by a high degree of formalization and impersonality, the primary group doggedly persists and is indeed often controlling. In a famous study of acculturation in Israel, Katz and Eisenstadt discovered that the much maligned bus driver often entered into all kinds of personal relations with the new immigrants from Africa and Asia who did not know how to ride a bus.

The problem therefore is not so much to describe the demise of the primary group in a contractual society, but rather to describe how primary group experience persists in such a society. The question is not the demise of community but rather its unexpected survival.

From this perspective we can see that to some extent the discussion is foreclosed if our term of comparison is the peasant society of agrarian Europe. This kind of community does not exist any more and apparently cannot exist in complex, specialized industrial society. It may have had its advantages but, to be perfectly honest, it was also a pretty stagnant, narrow, parochial community. If reading the life of St. John Vianney accomplishes nothing else, it should at least persuade us that Ars was no bargain as a community

In any case, this kind of parish has had its day. The argument about whether the modern parish is an association or a community is largely a waste of time. The proper question is rather to what extent a given parish offers satisfying primary group experiences to a substantial part of its membership. It may well be time to call a moratorium on the argument over community (or at least send it back to France) in favor of more realistic discussion of the type of primary group experience a parish should be providing. This would be far more realistic than lamenting our inability to reproduce the continuity of, let us say, rural Ireland.

Several comments about the contemporary parish are immediateely in order. First of all, religious community does not necessarily imply active participation in the parish as an organization. Admittedly the parish has an official structure which is centered around the rectory, the school, the hall, and the church. However, Lenski has demonstrated that one can be very much a member of the Catholic socio-religious group — the community — as far as values, friends, marriage partners, and beliefs go, without participating actively in formal religious exercises. There apparently exists an informal Catholic community in a neighborhood much as there is an informal community in an industrial plant.

One might even theorize that just as in the plant the informal community has more influence over the lives of the people than the formal, so the same thing may be true of a neighborhood. The informal connections between Catholics may be more important in shaping their lives and their values than the formal connections with the rectory. Such a possibility offers an area for some highly promising investigations. (In my own study of an upper middle class country club I found that Catholics played golf most of the time with other Catholics and were more inclined to play with Catholics from their own parish, even if they were not particularly active in parish affairs.) It is time that our theorizing stop identifying the parish with the clergy.

Secondly, it is perfectly obvious that many, many parishes—be they old national parishes or new suburban ones—provide all kinds of primary group experience for their members who may happen to desire such experience. Furthermore such parishes strive constantly to involve other parishioners in such relationships who are not in them presently and apparently do not desire to be involved.

More than this cannot reasonably be expected in urban society. No organization in our culture can count on the active participation of the majority of its members, much less all of them. What is required is that the organization have enough of its members involved so that the job it has set for itself may be accomplished. From this point of view the goal of the parish is not to involve everyone, but rather to involve enough so that the parish's task may, at least in some fashion, be efficiently accomplished.

Thirdly, we ought to realize that primary group experience is not a good in itself. The mere involvement of people in activity connected with the parish is not the *summum bonum*. A number of parishes have highly organized primary group networks (and could be called "communities" in this restricted sense) and yet fail as parishes because their members are so concerned with the activity that they lose sight of the goals, so committed to their own neighborhood (usually suburban) that they could not care less about the rest of the world. It is just possible that in our frantic concern to reconstruct the parish "community" we are building a monster—a parish composed of diligent, active, "community minded" people who are so "parochial" that they cannot see beyond the borders of their parish.

What is required is not just primary group experience but primary group experience oriented toward the needs of the Church. Such a statement borders on being a truism, yet one wonders how often it is honored in practice.

Fourthly, it seems pretty clear that many of the battles the Church must fight cannot be waged on the parochial level. Problems of the mass media, economic and social relations, racial justice, international peace, the underdeveloped countries—none of these are within the scope or the competence of the parish. The Church needs and needs rather desperately a vast assortment of techniques to meet the challenges of the twentieth century, and the parish is simply not suited for many of these techniques. The parish can no longer be relied upon as the only or even the major level at which the Church is engaged. The pious legend that the parish priest is the only priest really on the front lines should be forever put to rest.

However, to say that there are some things the parish cannot do is not to say that it can do nothing, although this distinction is often ignored in the argument about the future of the parish. Indeed a good case might be made for the argument that if the parish does not do its specific job extraordinarily well, then none of the other levels of the apostolate can hope to survive for very long.

It would be easy to get involved in an argument as to whether the parish is a natural or a supernatural community. Such a discussion would, I suspect, be pointless. It must of course be both; it cannot be one without the other. Grace builds on nature and nature prepares the way for grace. The parish can do its liturgical and formational tasks (which I am about to suggest are its main functions) well only if there is some sort of natural base. And if liturgy and formation are done the way they should be, the natural community should draw closer together.

In fact, one might even suggest that the secret could be to find what the informal communities of Catholics are within a parish, and use these as the basis of worship and formation instead of trying to impose a formal structure from the top.

What is necessary is not so much that the parish stop doing the things that it is doing though perhaps some could be discarded) but that it do them in a different fashion and for a different reason. The parish should look on itself as a feeder organization, sending people into other areas of the apostolate of the Church. It must, of course, provide for its own organizational needs, but it must not conceive of itself as an end. It must realize that it exists to service the larger Church rather than to be serviced by it. It provides the apostolic formation and the sacramental and liturgical fortification necessary that the Church may have a steady stream of dedicated clergy and laity fighting battles in other areas which are now being lost by default because of the absence of trained and motivated Christians.

This is not to imply the unimportance of the parish, but rather to give it profound new importance. It is from the point of view of the parish as basically a formational and liturgical center that one must judge the benefit and relevance of a given form of primary group experience on the parochial level.

(Obviously this is a theoretical discussion. The

functions described are the *ideal* functions of the modern parish. In the practical order, many parishes, in the mission neighborhoods of a large city for example, are so involved in staying alive that the ideal must remain a remote one. It is not demanded that every parish come close to the ideal, but that the ideal remain the ultimate goal, even if unrealizable in the present situation.)

One particularly obvious fact about the parish seems to be frequently overlooked in discussion: for most Catholics, during most of their lives, the parish is the only place where they are in formal contact with the Church. In any foreseeable situation, at least in this country, this fact will not be changed. Whether we like it or not, for most Catholics the parish will continue to be the Church, no matter how complex or sophisticated our super-parochial apostolate will become. Catholics—even those in influential positions in the land—will judge the Church by what they know best, the parish. No matter how impressive our super-parochial structure may and indeed must become, the only channel of influence we have to the average Catholic will be his parish.

It would seem to the present writer that our efforts should be devoted not so much to making the parish more like some ideal concept of what a community should be, much less to lamenting the demise of community, but rather to taking whatever primary group structure we have and opening it up to the needs of the Church. It is not a question of building community so we may worship, nor of worshiping so that we may have community, but rather of taking whatever community we have and teaching it how to worship and the meaning of worship so that it may go forth to meet the problems of the larger community. Our challenge, with some exceptions, is not to provide more primary group experience, but to turn the primary group structure we have to the service of the Body of Christ.

III. The Family and the Suburbs

The suburban migration is alleged to have produced a new type of husband, a new type of wife, a new type of parent, a new type of child. In this section these allegations are examined, and the prospects for the future are considered.

9

The Suburban Husband...
The Vanishing American

A considerable amount of tears have been shed in recent years over the sad plight of the American male —mostly by American males. We read that the breadwinner of the family is permitted to be just that and little else. He is molded into a condition of dependence by one generation of women so that he may serve as a slave for the next two generations. He is allowed to bring home his weekly pay check and perform all sorts of menial chores around the house, but the major decisions affecting his life and that of his family are made by his mother, then by his wife, and finally by his wife and daughters in concert. In the new American Matriarchy the male has become strictly a second-class citizen. What is worse, he doesn't seem to mind; in fact, it would appear that he rather enjoys the whole thing.

It is in the suburbs, we are informed, that this enslavement has become complete. With his countless household duties, from changing diapers to shopping at the supermarket, the suburban husband and father has become thoroughly domesticated. In fact, as he spends his few precious hours of free time in the evening working on Cub Scout committees or attending parent-teacher conferences, he seems to have surrendered completely not only to his wife but to his children as well. He has become the last of the hired help, a member of the new servant class.

This, then, is supposed to be the male animal—variety, 1962 American. But the picture, like so many other stereotypes of suburban culture, is somewhat beside the point. Granted that there has been a considerable increase in the domesticity of the father, it by no means follows that he has abdicated his freedom. Until the causes of this domesticity are investigated we have no reason to say that he might not actually be looking for a new kind of freedom; that if he does not complain about drying dishes or going to little-league meetings or chaperoning teen-age dances, it might not be because he likes these things—or at least feels that he should like them.

The fact that modern man is quite familiar with housework hardly seems questionable. Various surveys show that a third of the husbands in the country do the dishes, clean house and look after the children, and more than half of them do a good deal of the family shopping. The Gallup poll insists that 62 per cent do the dishes some of the time and 40 per cent help with the cooking. In New York 87 per cent of the young men between 21 and 29 help with the housework. But statistics are hardly necessary. A mere glance around any suburb of a Saturday morning is sufficient proof. The man of the house must be a part-time electrician, plumber, carpenter, house painter, landscaper, gardener, bricklayer (for the barbecue pit), mechanic and, in some cases, swimming-pool attendant. For a man to admit that he is not "handy" is almost as much a confession of failure as bankruptcy proceedings.

The suburban father is expected to take a profound interest in the rearing of the children whom he sees for only a few hours a day. In the multitude of suburban novels, a standard way of evoking "atmosphere" is to have two commuters converse on the railroad station platform about the Cub pack, or the forthcoming Little League championship, or next summer's father-son wiener roast or the plans to flood the tennis courts so their children will have a place to skate.

There is little question that these fictional conversations are authentic reflections of reality. Suburbanite fathers are almost compulsively interested in seeing that their children get every benefit possible, and the person who questions the wisdom of showering attention and advantages on the little ones is immediately suspected of communism or some other vile belief. If both father and mother are child-centered, the father is the more irrationally so—perhaps because his guilt feelings with relation to his children are more profound. Anyone who has watched fathers cheering at a grammar school football game is inclined to wonder whether a de-emphasis on juvenile sports might not prolong life—for parents.

The important point about the husband's new role as household servant and recreation supervisor is that he is not making policy in these areas—at least not normally. He is doing what his wife and children ask him to do or hint that he should do. He is a lesser member of the family bureaucracy, who executes decisions made while he is away at work. This is not because the family does not trust him to make decisions. Rather the reason seems to be that he does not particularly want to make them. He has had more than enough decisions to make during the working day. If someone else will relieve him of the responsibility of doing this at home, he will be more than happy to go along with whatever has been decided. His laissez faire attitude toward the family creates a vacuum into which his wife and children must move, and his feelings of guilt about not making decisions forces him to go along with what the rest of the family wants. As one perhaps mythical suburban male puts it, "In our family my wife makes the little decisions and I the big ones. She decides where we are going to live, where we will go on vacations, how we will spend our money, when we will get a new car, what schools we will send our children to, whether we can afford a color TV— that sort of thing. And I decide what stand the family will take on major problems, such as foreign aid, nuclear testing, inflation, corruption in government, and the next Presidential election."

These, then, are the signs of the new matriarchy; but before we view them as evidence of the final abdication of the masculine half of the American nation, we ought to add a few qualifications. First of all, we may be permitted to wonder if the matriarchy is anything really new. The sort of "little" decisions that the wife in the last paragraph made seem to have been in the feminine domain during the history of most of what passes for civilization. Women may possibly have changed their techniques for exercising influence in these areas, they may have become less subtle and more open in their demands, but whether there has been any substantial change in recent decades might still need considerable proof. Within the memory of man, husbands have expected from their wives exactly what the President expects from the Senate—advice and consent (with plenty of the former and much less of the latter).

Secondly, the causes of the new position of the father in the home go much deeper than the mere feminine desire to have her own way. The same social forces that brought about the suburban expansion have molded a special kind of suburban father and husband.

There are many causes for the changed relationship between husband and wife, between father and family. The GI-Bill culture in which wives supported husbands who went to school and watched the children after school hours, the new fashion for large and quickly acquired families which increases the amount of work a wife must do in the early years of marriage; the vanishing of the domestic help which once accompanied suburban home ownership; the "do it yourself" craze; the high cost of construction work; the thousand and one unexpected things that can go wrong with a new house; the invention of power tools and other electronic gadgets before which the male ego is helpless; the forty-hour week—all these have contributed to the domestication of husbands.

But a much deeper factor is at work. As we have indicated in previous chapters, Suburbia is in large part an escape from the inhumanity and ugliness of the industrial environment into a new sense of community found in the suburbs, which can offer some of the values the small peasant villages furnished to our ancestors. In the same fashion the new domesticity is at least in part an escape for the male from the competitive rigors of his occupational world. In the intimacy of family life, he finds refuge from the impersonal "rat race" of earning a living.

It is one of the cardinal points of current American folklore that happiness can be found only in the joys of marriage and family. The world of business and profession is represented as hectic, heartless and often vicious. Despite the new emphasis on teamwork and committee management, competition is still fierce. To be a success one must not only work arduously and competently, but also impress one's superiors with one's poise and personality. The road to success is rough and rocky, and very few make it to the end. One must keep one's eye constantly on the goal—the top—and also on one's fellow strivers who might elbow one off the road. Beneath the lively good fellowship of the expense account lunch or the golf foursome, the deadly serious business of being a success takes a tremendous toll in strain and tension. In our business culture the drive for success is almost unquestioned and the rewards in prestige and power for those who get to the top of the heap are thought to be tremendous.

But there are few rewards or satisfactions, other than financial, immediately obvious to those who are still striving for the top or those who have resigned themselves to never reaching it. For these, folklore tells us, the family is a place where they can cease to be cogs in the monstrous machine and once again become human beings. Our culture demands that a man be ambivalent about his career. He should strive to be successful at it, yet he should recognize that the true satisfactions are to be found elsewhere. In the suburban era, the striving may not have become any less frantic, but the attempt to find emotional satisfaction elsewhere has become far more prevalent and far better organized.[1]

So the vigorous family life of the suburbs is to some extent an attempt to recapture the joys of family unity which were once so readily available to most men. But just as the suburbs cannot escape the city, so the man cannot escape his occupational world. In fact, the farther he moves physically from the source of his internal tension, the greater becomes the conflict between home and work. If it was difficult to be a business executive and an apartment house father, it is far more difficult to be an Organization Man and a suburban father. Much more is expected of the father in the suburbs, but the conflict between the qualities required of a breadwinner and the qualities required of the head of a family has not become appreciably less acute. In fact, the rigors of commuting may possibly intensify the conflict. Suburban man immerses himself in family living because he honestly believes this is the way

[1] The contrast between business success and family happiness is a staple of modern fiction. John P. Marquand's *So Little Time* and *Point of No Return* are the forerunners of the current crop of suburban novels. Unfortunately, as we noted in commenting on the most famous of these—*The Man in the Gray Flannel Suit*—the choice in life is not nearly so obvious or uncomplicated as it is in fiction. The most popular novels today are about suburbs, advertising men, or college professors. It was a "natural" for some writers to put two of these elements together and start to write about the advertising man who must choose between the "mink-lined rat trap" and the family and home in the suburb. If an enterprising young novelist can combine all three elements and write about a college professor who lives in a suburb and does Motivation Research for an advertising firm, he will have found a formula as surefire as Lincoln's doctor's dog.

to happiness. Yet the attitudes and techniques he has developed for success in the business world make it extremely difficult for him to enjoy his new family chores or even to do them well. If he lets his wife make so many family decisions, one of the reasons may be that he is afraid he is unequipped to make the right ones, and in fact prone from his work experiences to make the wrong ones. He may be right.

The polarity between home and work has become so much a part of our culture that we tend to think it is in the nature of things. However, in other cultures such polarity was nonexistent, or at least very rare. When the family farm was the main economic unit, all the economic and social forces in a culture conspired to cement family unity and make it easy for the father to play his dual role of head of the family and main breadwinner. In fact, the father probably would have doubted that there was any duality to the role. It is a truism to say that modern industrial living has put all sorts of stresses on the family; but the extent of those stresses becomes glaringly apparent when we see the suburbanite father try valiantly to become a fully participating member of his family. If at times he feels uncomfortable or makes a fool of himself or fails completely, it should not astonish us. What is astonishing is that he succeeds as well as he does.

There are at least three obstacles to harmonizing home and work. First, even in these days of the forty-hour week, there is little time available to spend with the family. Secondly, when the father does arrive home, he is usually so exhausted, physically and mentally, that it often requires sheer heroism to be even mildly human to his wife and children. Finally, the goals, the ethics, the methods and the techniques of occupational life are vastly different from those of the family. It requires profound psychological adjustment to move each day from a world of rationality, money, and competition to a world of sentiment, generosity and co-operation. Since most of his waking day is spent in the former world, it is hard for its preoccupations not to influence his activities in the latter.

Obviously the theory stated in the last few paragraphs needs some qualifications. The extreme of opposition between home and work is sometimes noticeably lessened. The type of work, the personality of the father, the age of the couple, the amount of family debt—all these can cause considerable variation and modification in the degree of opposition. Some men make the transition from the occupational world to the family world with very little difficulty, while others find it much harder to make an adjustment. In no case is the opposition based necessarily on the lack of ethics in business life; even if a given occupational field is most ethical, its style of operation is still greatly different from the style demanded of the family.

The life of the male suburbanite is complicated by the fact that, for all his complaints about it, he probably likes his job. It may be a rat race, but he likes to race; it may be a battle, but he rather enjoys the battle. Folklore tells him he should get his main satisfactions at home and he may even feel that this is true, that he is happiest with his family. Yet the business world is in his blood. The urge to excel in what society in general considers to be the most important of natural activities is strong indeed. He may want the family to be the center of his life and to some extent it is; but the lure of the "big game" of business is much like that of the sea on the sailor. It is not particularly easy to say "no" to this attraction. For, in truth, many a man feels much more at home on his job than he does at home. He may not think he likes the job, but he has been trained for it from his early years and cannot get away from it.

This ambivalence is at the center of suburban man's problems. He must live in two vastly different worlds, worlds much farther apart psychologically than physically. Nor is this situation likely to change. We are not going to return to the family farm, for all its advantages; it had inconveniences that we are not interested in recapturing. The suburban attempt to create a new and generally satisfactory form of family life in an industrial society has not been a complete success; but it is not an experiment that is going to be abandoned in the foreseeable future. Many developments must still be made; for, just as the suburb cannot be an escape from the city, so domesticity cannot be an escape from the tensions of the occupational world. If the suburb is to be safe, the whole city must be transformed; so too, if the new domesticity is to be truly rewarding, a considerable change might be required in occupational life, or at least in man's approach to his occupational life. Such a change will be extremely difficult. For the occupation is a legitimate and important vocation. It is part of God's plan for an individual and one of the means of his sanctification. A man should not try to escape from it, but if he is to find true happiness in it, his attitudes toward his work must undergo substantial alteration. As of now, the precise nature of this humanization and Christianization of occupational life is not, it must be confessed, immediately apparent.

And yet, this humanization of executive work may well be one of the gravest social and spiritual challenges of our age. If our economic system is to function well, it would seem that almost impossible demands will be made on the group of men who hold executive positions in the corporate hierarchy—or at least those near the summit of that hierarchy. Apparently more and more young people are thinking twice before making that kind of commitment to The Corporation. Unless The Corporation finds a way to lessen the competitive rigors of its executives' lives, it may eventually have difficulty in recruiting men who are willing to struggle for the summit.

Yet can the competition for success be appreciably weakened without the system falling apart? Does not the struggle to move ahead furnish necessary motivation for the constant expansion and improvement of our economy? If the executive life were made much easier, would not our system begin to stagnate?

There are no easy answers to these questions. Perhaps the beginnings of a solution might be found in the concept of "vocation." I would doubt that there are rewards of money or power sufficient to compensate the corporate executive for the demands which are made on him. A new motivation must be added to the competition-for-success motive which is urged so strongly today. It is certainly not impossible to view the corporate bureaucracy as an extremely important form of public service and indeed a vocation. As a matter of fact, studies of bureaucratic structure seem to show that the more this idea of public service is present, the more efficiently a bureaucratic structure will operate.[2] To say that the motivation of public service might help to Christianize and humanize the work of the suburban executive is not to say that most of the public service propaganda of the modern corporation is to be taken at face value. However, what began as a sophisticated form of public relations might well end as a way of life for the corporation if it should prove to promote the morale and efficiency of its most important personnel. The ever increasing emphasis upon good community relations for the company shows a fruitful field for development.[3] That the corporation has been developing a conscience is not a particularly new discovery, but that this conscience might be necessary if it is to get their best efforts from its executives of the future is a relatively recent and extremely significant insight.

2 Peter Blau, *Dynamics of Bureaucracy* (Chicago: University of Chicago Press, 1955).

3 Wayne Hodges, *Company and Community* (New York: Harper, 1958).

10

The Suburban Wife...
Who Needs Her?

If the influence of the father in the family is declining, it would seem natural enough to assume that the power of the mother is gaining. The same mass media which have been lamenting the decline of the father (as noted in the last chapter) have not hesitated to make this deduction and to turn to the problems of the supposed new ruler in the American family. In fact, it has become quite fashionable in recent years for the top-circulation magazines to devote a whole issue to the "problem of American woman." The picture these magazines portray for us is not a bright one.

Roles in marriage, we are told, are being reversed. Wives are becoming more masculine, more domineering; husbands are becoming less male and more passive. A few generations ago women, for one reason or another, began to revolt against the secondary places assigned them in society. They demanded equal educational, political, and occupational rights with men. Eventually they got them. They have become equals with the male in most forms of social activity. They are emancipated from the old-fashioned notions of the Victorian age. They have taken their rightful place in society, whether it be in writing advertising copy, running for Congress or flying jets. Even those who have chosen marriage for their careers are surrounded by so many labor-saving gadgets that they are free forever from the drudgery of housework.

Yet, according to the journalists, the American woman is not happy with her new-found freedom. She seems to be afraid, anxious, frustrated. She has almost everything her grandmother could possibly have wanted and yet is far from satisfied. Her basic fear, we are told, is of emptiness. School, society, and machines have appropriated many of her traditional functions. Life seems to be without meaning for her much of the time. As a result she seeks escape in neurosis or alcohol or, more rarely, in infidelity. For all her new power in the family, the wife is somehow dissatisfied and unhappy.

Having stated the problem with enough gripping and concrete details to appeal to the emotions of the female element in their audience, the popular magazines proceed to bring their surveys to a pious conclusion by claiming that the American woman is beginning to adjust to her "interesting new life" and that her "awakening sense of responsibility" to the world around her promises great things for the future. This sort of conclusion—half sociology and half soap opera—is then backed up by a small collection of examples of women who are superb in the areas of life in which they are involved—be it politics, medicine, scientific research, advertising, motherhood, widowhood, or social service.

This analysis of the American woman is not something thought up by a few clever magazine editors. It is rather a popularization of what a good many social scientists and psychiatrists have been saying for some time. There seems to be something about contemporary culture which makes life particularly hard for women. The speed and harshness of modern society seem to confuse women even more than these factors confuse men. Naturally enough, not all women are unhappy or frustrated, just as not all men find the contrast between job and home difficult to tolerate. Our country, city and suburbs alike, abounds with happy, well-adjusted, non-neurotic woman (and men); nevertheless there does seem to be an increase in the amount of dissatisfaction and anxiety among the female half of the population. If at least one-fourth of the alcoholics in the country are women, it is safe to say that the social scientists and popular journalists have hit on a real problem. What is the matter with the American woman? With so much of the physical misery gone from her life, why has her emotional misery increased?

There are several different answers offered, none of which excludes the others. One theory sees woman's problem as basically the same as that of her husband—the conflict between home and career. Most American women today work before they are married, a good many continue to work until the first child comes, and a considerable number continue to work even after that. (One-fourth of the labor force is female.) In the case of the working wife, the tension between family and job would be similar to that of her husband except that it would probably be more severe because society still feels that a woman is better off in the home. Her guilt feelings on account of "neglecting" her family would be more intense.

In the American form of capitalism, the economic order is assumed to be the really important one. Business and profession constitute the part of life that really matters. Despite the new mythology of domesticity, the American subconscious still values the successful businessman more than it does anyone else. (One never makes the cover of *Time* for being a successful father.)

The female half of the population is not immune to this value system, especially when most women have spent at least a few years in some corner (and perhaps a big corner) of the world of careers. Since a woman's place is still thought to be in the home, the successful career woman who gives up her place in the business world to settle down to family life is normally admired. Nevertheless, everyone feels (with the possible exception of her husband) that she has made an almost heroic sacrifice. She has given up interesting work to make a home and has lost her precious equality with men. She has taken a somewhat inferior job for which she has little training or aptitude. She has given up her place in the competitive struggle for success. Of course she expects rewards for her sacrifice, and when marriage does not turn out to be quite what she thought it would be she feels disappointed and perhaps even cheated. She finds herself envying her husband the maneuverability, the excitement, the challenge, the variety of the "Big Game" of the business world while she is consigned to the narrowness and monotony of being a *hausfrau*.

A second explanation which is often advanced closely approximates the first, but it stresses the educational preparation of woman. In this day of co-education, there is little difference between the schooling of men and women. Even though a girl fully intends to spend most of her life in a kitchen, her education is still as career-oriented as her brother's. Except for the "vocationalism" of Home Economics, few schools make a pretense of training women for their roles as wife and mother. Hence, when these roles are thrust upon them, girls are apt to feel that their education was wasted; that there is no opportunity for them to continue the development of their intellects, and no point in it. Hence they let their intellectual processes stagnate and feel guilty as well as cheated.

There is probably a good deal of validity in this explanation; although I think that those who advance it often miss the basic point. Since most education today is oriented toward careers, neither boys nor girls value the development of the intellect for its own sake. Lack of interest in the good, true and beautiful is by no means limited to the housewife. A truly liberal education which awakened the curiosity, developed the sensitivities, and broadened the vision would not be wasted on a girl planning marriage. Indeed, there probably could be no better preparation for marriage. It seems to me that half-education rather than education might be the cause of unhappiness in marriage. A course in Dante or European History or Karl Marx might, in the long run, make for a happier housewife (and businessman, for that matter) than all the sewing and cooking (or Fabrics and Dietetics) courses in the world. In any walk of life there is no substitute for disciplined intelligence.

A third explanation, again closely related to the first two, is that the American wife feels that her husband is losing interest in her despite his often pathetic attempts to be an active family man. She resents having to share him with the corporation. She dislikes the feeling that she is playing second fiddle to a briefcase. It would be far easier to cope with another woman than with General Motors. She gets the impression that all her husband really wants is someone who will provide a few hours of peace, order, serenity, and comfort for him while he recoups his strength for the return to his first love—the job. How can she think that her husband really loves her when it seems that he has to force himself to give even minor attention to her problems and those of their children?

A final explanation incorporates parts of the other three and seems to the present writer, at least, the best yet offered. A woman's main need is to be needed, and the tragedy of the modern woman is that she is increasingly becoming unnecessary. In an agricultural society the woman was an integral part of the economic unit. She and her husband shared the responsibility for seeing that the farm was a successful one. Her contributions to the economic welfare of the family were necessary and obvious. She was the main educator even after the children had reached the age of six. She was the principal domestic worker. Her efforts and co-operation were essential to her husband; without her he would literally be powerless. The *mulier fortis* of the Bible, busy with her countless household and economic chores, was a real credit to her husband when he sat with the nobility of his community. There was little thought of her being an ornament whose charm and personality furthered her husband's career. She was needed and needed badly. Her life might have been a hard one, but it was never insignificant.

Certainly, much of this has changed. The schools (including the kindergarten and nursery school) have taken over much of the education of children; the secretary and stenographer have replaced the wife as her husband's economic assistant; a wide variety of mechanical devices have lessened her contribution to domestic labor and, if her husband's income is ample, part-time servants can be found to eliminate practically all such labor. This is not to say that she has nothing to do; for she has, especially when the children are still young. But so much of the work seems inconsequential and unimportant; it is the sort of thing that almost anyone can do and in a few years almost any machine *will* do. The wife has the feeling that her husband does not really need her very much. If she senses that she is only a marginal part of his life, it might be because she is of only marginal importance.

This could possibly be one explanation of the current baby boom. Bearing and raising children are among the very few things left that a wife can do for her husband. Devoting her whole life to their offspring is a way of showing her love for her husband and can even become an eventual substitute for his affection. If so many American children are smothered by "momism," the reason might be that they are all "Mom" has left.

The real problems begin, according to this theory, when the children are raised, or even when the youngest is safely away in school. The free time that one part of the woman has always wanted has at last come, and she does not know what to do with it. The gnawing feeling of being unnecessary can cause serious emotional disturbance at this stage. The full magnitude of the problem becomes apparent when we realize that today the average husband and wife have fourteen years more of marriage ahead of them after the last child is married—as opposed to the minus-one-year of fifty years ago. What precisely is there left for a wife to do?

How does the suburban wife and mother vary from this pattern? We could not expect much of a variation, since the analyses and theories presented in this chapter are obviously dealing with the American middle class (It would be interesting to spectulate on why so much that has been written on marriage and family problems has come out of a middle-class context. Certainly the working class—if one may be pardoned the expression—has its share of family problems too.) Suburbia is little more than a prolongation and a development of middle-class patterns that already exist.

At first glance, we might be tempted to think that suburban wives should be happier since they have more earthly possessions than most of their sisters or cousins in the big city. As one suburban wife said, "If they are not satisfied here, where will they be satisfied? Yet material possessions do not necessarily satisfy all human needs. The factors contributing to anxiety and bitterness seem to be even stronger in the suburbs. This does not mean that all or even a majority of suburban wives are unhappy in their marriages or doomed to feel unneeded and unnecessary. However, it does mean that there are strains and tensions which can readily make for frustration and that many suburban wives at least to some extent do succumb to such strains and tensions.

The suburban wife is likely to be better-educated, and to have been more deeply and more successfully involved in business life before her marriage. Her husband will probably be away from home more (if only because of time spent commuting), and more fully committed to his work. The contrast between the drabness and monotony of her routine and the excitement of his becomes more evident as he climbs the ladder to success. Cultural facilities (with the exception of shopping plazas) are farther away. The variety and interest of a cosmopolitan area are absent. Labor-saving devices will be more prevalent than in the city. If a wife is tempted to feel unnecessary, there is little in suburban life which will make her feel different and much which will confirm her suspicion. She may have greater responsibilities with the family, but this is merely because her husband is too busy to be really interested. Even the frantic social life of many suburbs very quickly becomes a burden; there is even less time for her and her husband to share their love. The hard, brittle heroine of suburban novels may not be typical, but unfortunately there are too many women who are forced to build up all sorts of defense mechanisms and self-deceptions to keep from facing the apparent blighting of their dreams.

"Togetherness" and the New Domesticity are taken to be the answers to these frustrations. The quest for community is not limited to suburban man alone. His wife wants it just as much as, perhaps more than, he does. To some degree this quest has been successful and the "doing it together" of the suburbs has brought a greater degree of happiness to many marriages. But suburban community is still partially an artificial revolt against the evils of industrialism. That both the men and women of the suburbs have begun to feel the need for more community in their married life is a most encouraging sign. But there is no reason to be certain that the means they have chosen to attain this community will not be self-defeating. The Catholic family movements which stress that husband and wife together are lay missionaries with a duty and opportunity to serve their fellow men may point the way to a constructive family revival in the suburbs. In joint works of charity and social justice husbands and wives may not only enkindle enthusiasm for the service of society; they may even re-enkindle enthusiasm for each other.

The idea of husband and wife together serving the common good might fit in with the notion of the executive vocation discussed at the end of the last chapter. The wives of doctors seem to find it a little easier to put up with the frequent absence of their husbands, because they feel that by patiently bearing such difficulties they are helping in their husband's work of aiding others. When a girl marries a doctor it is assumed that she knows what she is getting into.

If the corporation executive could be thought of as a similar kind of public servant, his wife's morale might be considered improved. This in turn could lessen his guilt feelings over "neglecting" his family. Should the wife be able to join in this service, even in a small way, the family relationship would improve still more. Nor should this be particularly difficult, especially when the husband works for a corporation which feels that involvement in community affairs beyond the immediate needs of the company is a good thing for its executives.

The application of the theology of work in this and in the preceding chapter certainly is not a panacea, nor is it meant to be anything more than an indication of possible development. If such development does take place, it may prove considerably easier in the future for the Catholic suburbanite to bear witness to Christ in the temporal order.

11

The Young People of Suburbia...
Not Exactly "Shook-Up"

Few human beings can resist the temptation to peer into the future. When presented with a revolutionary social development, man becomes immensely curious as to where the new phenomenon is going. In twentieth-century America, as a matter of fact, what a trend is leading to is normally a far more important question than where it came from. Hence the tremendous interest in the future of Suburbia. What will the next generation of suburbanites be like? What kind of children are growing up in the post-war suburbs? In what directions are the suburban teenagers going? In a world of Dewey and Freud, are we raising a generation of juvenile delinquents? Are the young people of the suburbs as 'shook-up' as their press releases seem to indicate? The answers to these questions, it is to be feared, are considerably less dramatic than the questions. There seem to be good strong reasons to believe that, wonder of wonders, the suburbanite children are not very much different from their parents, certainly not worse than the generation which went before and not appreciably better.

According to Dwight MacDonald, in his recent series in *The New Yorker,* the emergence of the teenager as a distinct social group is relatively recent. Since World War II, the teen-agers have become a subculture with its own folkways and value systems. They are now a special market, with clothes, food and drink, typewriters, magazines, music, movies ("Hot Rod Rumble," "Juvenile Jungle," "How to Make a Monster," etc.), and Motivation Research designed especially for them. In fact, MacDonald thinks that many teen-agers, with a personal disposable income of over five hundred dollars a year, have more money to spend at their whim than do parents. Hence he argues that teen-agers are rapidly becoming the fashion leaders of our country. Certainly, they rule supreme in the area of movies and AM radio, and if the Ivy League styles mean anything, they seem to be taking over in the clothing field. Instead of being a matriarchy, the United States may well be on its way to becoming a "teen-archy."

Beyond all doubt, teen-agers are a remarkably independent lot. The weakening of family ties, the working mother and the father who may hold two jobs, the disturbances of the last war, the financial independence of a younger generation with nine billion dollars to spend on itself each year, the maneuverability of a car—all these have given the youth of today far more freedom than was enjoyed in days gone by. If we are to judge by the newspaper headlines, they are using this freedom to make the city streets unsafe for anyone not skilled in the gentle art of the "rumble." The rebellious teen-agers of today seem to be the younger brothers and sisters of the Beat Generation, rebels without a cause who are not particularly looking for any cause besides the sacred standard of Rock and Roll. In the minds of many solid and substantial citizens "teen-agers" has become synonymous with "juvenile delinquent."

Obviously such a notion is not altogether accurate. Even in rumble-prone New York, only 3 per cent of the juveniles ever get into trouble with the police. But the identification of "teen" and "delinquent" is not exactly the important question. Hardly an older generation in history has failed to despair of its offspring. The new element in the present situation is the vast freedom of the younger generation—a freedom unparalleled in middle-class history. A proper question to pose would be about the use of this new freedom. Will the younger generation mount a serious and prolonged rebellion against the goals and values of its parents? As far as the majority of the youth of Suburbia is concerned, the answer must be a prompt "no."

Even MacDonald, who is somewhat "shook-up" about the younger generation, admits that, after the years of the teen revolution, the younger generation very quickly settles down during its early twenties to be "nice young people" with a brood of children and the most approved type of ranch house. One need only add that in Suburbia the duration of the revolt is often so short as to make the fact of revolution questionable. Without realizing it, parents have become skilled practitioners of the art of human relations. Shrewdly conceding more freedom to their offspring, they have in the process made certain that the children shall internalize the goals of our culture. Parents may not be treated with as much respect as in former years, but the values of parental society are accepted without question. If teen-agers are rebels without a cause, it is often because in our most affluent of societies there is really no point in rebellion. The kids want what their parents already have, and to attain this in modern America one need not rebel; hard work will be just as effective and much less costly. Our youth may appear brash, but all the while they are being fitted for their own tailor-made gray flannel suits.

It has long since ceased to be news that American college students have become extremely conservative (this despite the threat of the Communists, socialists, atheists, Keynesians and other odd types which we hear have taken over our college faculties). Every Sunday supplement reader in the country has been told that the "flaming youth" of the modern campus wants to do little more than have a good job, settle down with a wife and family, and attend the church of his choice on Sunday. Balance has succeeded success as a life goal. The career is important, but not nearly as important as the family, and only 9 per cent think that helping others will be one of the main causes of happiness during their life. If there is any difference between this sort of aim and the standard professed by the present generation of suburban adult, it is not immediately evident.[1]

How does the suburban teen-ager fit into this picture of national conservatism? There have not been many studies of the children whose conscious years began after the end of the last war, but on the basis of my own observations, it would seem that suburban teen-agers settle down to the serious business of being a well-balanced success during their junior year of high school. Whatever rebellion is going to take place is over by this time, if it ever really had much of a chance.

The suburban youngster is extremely domestic. His family life has been, by and large, pleasant, and he is eager to get his own little domestic community going. "Going steady" and early marriages are probably the teen-age manifestation of the ever present suburban "quest for community." Yet the youthful suburban male realizes that he should not get too much involved until he is able to support a family with the kind of job necessary for a happy family life. Domesticity is a goal that must often be deferred if it is to be enjoyed in the fashion which his parents have shown him is most satisfying. The suburbanite learns

[1] Yet college graduates still verbalize idealistic goals. In a recent study in which the author took part, the most popular occupational values among college graduates were 'a chance to be helpful to others' and 'opportunities to be original and creative.' Money and security were far down the list. Perhaps it is not so much a question of idealism being dead in modern young people—as this chapter implies—but of there being no obvious outlet for it. More on this problem should appear in a forthcoming book on college graduates which Sheed & Ward will pubish in 1963.

at a very tender age of the conflict between home and occupation.

Our young friend is very studious. His parents will tolerate all sorts of "progressive" experiments in their high schools so long as their children do well in the College Board examinations; but if a school superintendent gets so tied up in promoting "life adjustment" that he forgets about the academic preparation for higher education, he had better start looking for a professorship at some teachers' college. Teen-age suburbanites are much more likely to get into trouble with their parents because of bad marks than because of the more highly publicized forms of juvenile mischief. Deprivation of the family car is the all-important sanction which can be invoked at the slightest sign of a slackening of effort. Off-the-street programs are the last thing in the world needed in a suburban community on weekday evenings during the school year. I still remember the shock I experienced when I realized that I had not seen a teen-ager on the streets of my neighborhood after dark from one end of the winter to the other. In fact, it has proved most difficult to get them into the streets even for church activities like YCS or evenings of recollection. First things come first, and studies are first. With all his studiousness, the young suburbanite is not particularly interested in the things of the intellect for their own sake. Grades, credits, courses and suchlike are important things in his life because of their connection with his eventual career and the family the career will make possible; but he is not very curious about the world of the mind. No one would dream of calling him an "egghead."

He is interested in sports and probably plays at some of them—especially basketball; but he does not take sports as seriously as his cousins in the old neighborhood did. The Sunday afternoon softball doubleheaders which used to be community events of great importance have become things of the past. He is modest in victory and relatively undiscouraged in defeat. Sports are fun but strictly a minor thing in life. Above all, they must not be permitted to interfere with his studies. It is not at all unusual for a suburbanite star to turn down an athletic scholarship with the sage comment that he is not going to be a professional athlete and that training for his career comes before sports.

He knows the value of money. Even if his parents can afford to send him to college without his doing a day's work, he is expected to contribute to his own education. This is supposed to be part of his training. It started when, as a grammar school child, he had his first paper route so that he could "learn the value of money." "Crestwood Heights," by the way, is not the only place where parents drive their paper-delivering sons around their routes on sub-zero days. The image of the rich and "spoiled" young suburbanite squandering his parents' money in drunken idleness or wild automobile sprees is largely mythical. Money and time are both precious and must be spent wisely and well.

He is quiet, unimaginative, and, in the final analysis, docile. His wild flings are rather rare, although, like his parents, he may drink a little too much. For all his informality with adults, he seldom disagrees with them in matters of grave importance. In fact, it is not altogether unheard-of for his parents to decide exactly what courses he will take in school. But his parents run his life not so much by decree as by consultation. They no longer make his decisions for him. They "help" him to decide what he wants to do.

No one can accuse him of being an enthusiast—at least in the terms used in our discussion of enthusiasm in a following chapter. He is sophisticated, worldly-wise, and just a trifle cynical. There may be a few years in his middle teens when he has **big** dreams and noble ideas about serving humanity, but this youthful generosity does not last very long and is normally quite dead by the end of his first year in college. He believes in playing it "cool" and is no more interested in making a commitment to something that might interfere with his career than is his father. It is to be feared that he has become middle-aged far before his time.

For all his conservation and apparent poise, he is insecure. For he knows that he is expected to "do well" in his career. He is under no illusion that the battle will be easy. He is sure that it can be won by the strong and skilled. He knows that he has had, or will have had, all the training and background necessary for success. But he is not sure of himself. He does not know whether he has what it takes to meet the challenges he must face.

This uncertainty about himself and his abilities can be very frightening. Popular impressions to the contrary notwithstanding, teen-age is not a very happy or carefree time. Its worries, anxieties, and insecurities are a special torture to the suburbanite from whom so much is expected. Failure is always a possibility which is not too far around the corner.

Although his moral code might be somewhat more lax than that of his grandparents, the suburban teen-ager is usually religious. He believes in God, normally goes to church, and even prays when he needs something. If he is a Catholic, he receives the sacraments frequently. Of course religion is merely a compartment in his life, a group of things to be done instead of a way of doing all things, but in this he is not very different from his progenitors. He may slip a little in his religious practice when he gets into college, and may even have a few doubts about the whole institution of organized religion, but he is not going to lose his faith. Religion is too necessary a thing in his vision of a comfortable, stable world like the one he was raised in.

Thus far we have described the young suburbanite as a boy, but if we were to go back and change the gender of each third-person pronoun, few other alterations would be needed to make the paragraphs apply to girls. The "career" for a suburban girl will be her marriage, and she will be a "success" if her marriage is a "success." Studies might not be quite so important for her, but she is expected to have some sort of professional competence to fall back on if her husband's illness or death should make her the family breadwinner. College, at least for a few years, is essential for social poise, and probably for the acquiring of a husband. Development of the intellect is of even less importance for her. She will be much less interested in the world beyond her immediate ken than is her brother or boy friend; and when the wonderful day of days comes on which she can proudly announce to an eagerly waiting world that she is engaged, the rest of the human race can go up in a cloud of radioactive smoke for all she cares.

This, then, is the youth of Suburbia: friendly, serious, hardworking, intelligent. Few of them look like Elvis Presley or Jimmy Dean or their screaming admirers; fewer still remotely approach delinquency. If any criticism is to be leveled at them, it is that they are too conservative, too cynical, too "cool." What will Suburbia be like in twenty-five years? If these young people have anything to say about it, it won't be very much different from what it is now. For all their independence, they have bought their parents' "system," lock, stock and barrel.

Let us not be too quick to rejoice in this picture of youthful maturity. It is the function of the young to dream dreams, to infuse a little restlessness into society. When youth buys its parents' world completely, society should start to worry just a little. The young suburbanite might be a very fine son or daughter; but, to be perfectly honest, he (or she) is uninteresting and even slightly dull. One begins to yearn for somebody who wants to change the world, or who at least thinks that there are some things which need changing. Suburbia is turning out great numbers of good, solid, reliable young people; but the nation needs more than this if it is to survive. One must look hard in Suburbia to find youth who some day will be planners, poets, artists, philosophers, prophets, or saints. Yet without these "unadjusted" citizens no society can long survive. It is possible that Suburbia could do well with a little more teen-age rebellion.

Yet the picture is not altogether black (and here the author must rely entirely on personal observation). Poets, prophets and saints have never been a very large group in society. In fact, it is doubtful if they would ever make an appreciable difference in a statistical curve at any time in history. They have always had to face strong opposition from the culture of which they are a part; yet they seem to have thrived on it. Suburbia may yet produce some of this rare breed; perhaps in that 9 per cent who expect to get their main life-satisfaction out of helping others there is yet to be found a suburban version of Dante, St. Francis, or Thomas More. There need not really be too many; just a little bit of poetry, prophecy, and sanctity can go a long way. Perhaps even now the first stirrings can be heard; Suburbia is producing a few youngsters who aspire to be writers or artists, to serve actively in the lay apostolate, to devote part of their life to the foreign missions. Beneath the hard outer crust of suburban complacency the ferment of a saving remnant may already be at work. There are some signs that Suburbia is producing a few, but a significant few, "unadjusted" men and women. It had better.

IV. Suburban Humanism

An isolated man, one who has not become conscious of the ultimate objective link binding him to all other men before God, is an unawakened, immature, even a mutilated man.

DIETRICH VON HILDEBRAND: *Liturgy and Personality* [1]

[1] New York: Longmans, 1943.

Suburbia is part of the post-war world, a world different from any other period in American history. The chapters in this section portray some aspects of this world which have a profound influence on the suburban way of life and its problems—the quest for community and security, the refusal to get involved, the continuation of prosperity, the abundance of leisure and the power of the mass media. It is in a world where these factors are at work that Suburbia has appeared, and hence Suburbia is inevitably colored by their values. The concluding chapter of this section describes the threat which automation is beginning to pose to the suburban dream.

12

Conformity or Community

For many years it has been the fashion for after-dinner speakers to deplore the decline of American greatness. Countless thousands of business and professional men have been warned that measures such as social security or the seniority system threaten to destroy American incentive and ingenuity. Corporation executives have been urged to depart from the banquet table with a mission to spread the gospel of hard work and rugged individualism to a younger generation which has grown soft and allowed itself to be deceived by alluring promises of comfort and security. These talks have taken on something of the nature of a ritual to which no one really pays much attention; but within the last few years a new group of critics have arisen with a similar but much more sophisticated criticism of American life. They see the United States threatened with a new tyranny—the tyranny of the all-powerful group which demands total conformity from each of its members. Individual creativity, we are told, is being destroyed by the new American worship of the group. "Conformity" and "security" have become the magic words to explain all the ills of American society.

The critics make an extremely good case for their analysis. "Togetherness" has become a way of life as well as a clever advertising slogan. Families are urged to diet together, to go to "the church of their choice" together, to play together, to wear the same color bathrobes, to do their housework together, to paint pictures together. Husbands are told that their place is in the home, and they scarcely raise a sound in protest; they have become so adept at household chores that, as we have said, they are referred to as the new servant class. With his hands in dishwater and the apron strings firmly tied, the male achieves a happy domesticity which, together with his bridge and Cub Scout activity, shields him from the hard problems of the world outside the home.

Children are taught the values of the group from their earliest days. Their teachers no longer give grades or urge their pupils to academic competition. The teacher is not an instructor who imparts knowledge, but a "resource person" who "sparks sharing" and is very careful not to interfere with the dynamics of classroom groups by communicating opinions, attitudes, and ideas. The student, eager to advance in the mechanics of life adjustment, can take such subjects as "how to be liked," "how to get along with the crowd," "how to get closer to Dad." IBM machines which can record only "yes-no," "right or wrong" or "check one" answers determine whether the studious teen-ager will pass the dreaded College Board examinations; small wonder that the potential collegian is discouraged from thinking in terms of "maybe" or "there's something to be said for both sides." Distinctions such as these are beyond the comprehension of the calculating machine. Passing the examinations is all-important because only in college can a young American learn fully how to get along with his fellows.

The Group has taken over in business and professional worlds. The brilliant industrial autocrat has been replaced by committee management with its constant reports and counter-reports, its tons of memoranda and counter-memoranda. Financing a new project is no longer the work of a single financial genius like a Morgan, but rather the result of the co-operation of a large syndicate of investment bankers. Research is done no longer by a lonely, starving Edison or Bell, but by a well-fed group of paid scientists working on assigned projects. Planning is not the work of one man with uncanny hunches but rather the product of frantic group "brainstorming," a process wherein debate and criticism are ruled out and everyone tries to feel that the session is "like playing a game." Younger executives are chosen not so much for their powers of mind as for their ability to get along with people and for the "profile" that their personality tests reveal. In medicine, the single specialist is becoming a thing of the past, following in the footsteps of his lowly predecessor, the general practitioner. Group practice and the gigantic clinic have been found to be far more efficient. Joint research projects and interdisciplinary co-operation are the fashion on the university campuses. The "team spirit" is permeating our national government. Motivation Research and its spurious offspring, subliminal advertising, aim no longer at the isolated individual but at the "opinion makers" in the group. Political candidates are merchandised for their group appeal in the same fashion as are new automobiles. As we saw earlier, eminent observers claim that the "Protestant Ethic" of striving for success has been replaced by the "Social Ethic" of getting along with the group. "Inner-directed" man is yielding to the "other-directed," and the whole nation seems to be rejoicing in the change.

The happy theorists of group dynamics go their merry way, planning how group domination can expand in our society and bring harmony and happiness to us all—whether we want it or not. They experiment with their T-groups and their S-groups and their C-groups and brightly assure us that once they can overcome the problems of "semantics" and "communication" they will be able to bring us to a blessed nirvana of "agendaless groups" and "leaderless groups." To measure the degree of our happiness in this wondrous condition they have even developed the Harwald Groups Thinkometer, which measures the degree of unanimity in a group.

To prove the sorry effect of "groupism" the critics point to the recent studies of the present generation of collegians. The "hope of the future" are apparently a conservative—not to say stodgy—lot who expect little more out of life than a comfortable suburban domesticity and a job which will enable them to develop some of their social skills while not interfering too much with family happiness and security. To fight to the top, to serve mankind, to change the world — these are the farthest thoughts from their quiet, complacent minds.

So the critics of groupism rest their case. *Hamlet,* they observe, could not have been written by a committee, nor could a group have painted the *Mona Lisa* or designed the dome of St. Peter's. If there is a potential Shakespeare in our midst, he is writing ad copy on Madison Avenue. If there is a potential Abraham Lincoln, he is grinding out nonsense about Militant Liberty for the Defense Department. If there is a potential Edison, he is hamstrung by a group at the GE Research Center. If there is a potential St. Thomas Aquinas, he is busy counting noses so that the statistics in his doctoral dissertation will enable him to get a job teaching life adjustment to high school sophomores.

Thus speak the critics, and the thoughtful observer cannot help wondering whether theirs is a penetrating description of American society at mid-twentieth century or a cruel caricature. Have we Americans really lost faith in democracy, in the ability of a man to make his own decisions and to determine his own fate? Has the group really replaced the individual as the important unit in our society? Are we bound for some kind of enlightened collectivism?

There is no denying the increased importance of conformity as a cultural force in our society. Groupism is part of the spirit of the times. The criticism of the anti-groupists is in great part true; but, like many other brilliant sociological insights, it is not the whole truth. For the picture to be complete, certain qualifications must be added, the reasons behind the phenomenon must be investigated, and its possible merits must be assessed. One would think, to read some of the articles written on the subject, that conformism was something new. Actually it is as old as human nature. There was precious little room for creative individualism in the Greece of Socrates, the England of James I, or the America of Cotton Mather. Innovations or deviations from the norm have always been eyed askance by established society. Modern suburbanites did not invent conformism; it even may be debated whether they or the social critics are the ones to have rediscovered it. Perhaps it has always been part of American culture, but has become obvious only in our own day.

We might even question how many of our ancestors were rugged individualists in any true sense of the words. The pioneer spirit about which we hear so much characterized only a small minority of American society at any given time since the Revolution. Only a very few of the pioneers objected to settling down to a very quiet, conforming domesticity when they got a chance. Unless they were forced by economic adversity, only a very few shared Daniel Boone's legendary urge to keep moving.

As a matter of fact, most of our grandparents were poor, confused immigrants who hardly came close to the classic notion of the rugged individualist of the frontier. If they were rugged, it was because they had to be to survive the rigors of crossing the Atlantic and the miseries of nineteenth-century industrial society; if they were individualists, it was because it took them several years to realize that the only way to obtain their rights was to organize into groups for self-protection. Inner-directed men may have existed, they may have given society its tone, but, numerically speaking, they were few and far between. They may have left their mark on our nation's history, but they did so very often at the cost of great suffering for many of the ancestors of those who are being warned today about the danger of conformity.

There is no reason to glorify peasant society. It had its many faults, and its passing is by no means a tragedy. But it did meet certain human needs that modern industrialism has yet to satisfy. Stability, affection, personal loyalty, friendship, status, the esteem of one's fellows, a sense of belonging—the village culture was geared to serve these needs. Its traditional organized relationships offered the individual a moral and psychological center for his life. The emotional satisfaction of the face-to-face contacts of such groups as family, church, work group, and local community quieted deep and abiding human longings. There may have been great physical suffering in peasant society, but at least a man knew who he was and what was expected of him. His emotional world was a secure and uncomplicated one, no matter how grim his physical world might seem.

Immigration and industrialism destroyed the community of peasant culture. The world became vast and complicated. The village became the metropolis. Family, neighborhood and church had but minor roles to play in the progress of society. The individual was cut adrift in a lonely crowd with no visible place to cast anchor. More physical needs were being met than ever before, but some important psychological ones were being overlooked or ignored in the process. Modern man became isolated and rootless, without position, without status, without anything to which he could belong. Is it not possible for us to see in the migration to the suburbs, in the religious revival, in the emphasis on domesticity, in the rise of groupism, a vague and uncertain attempt of the grandchildren of the immigrants to recover some of the values left behind in the peasant villages of Europe? If this explanation be correct, it is certainly not enough merely to rail against the absurdities of "togetherness"; for "togetherness" is but a corruption of the natural human longing for community and a manifestation of a profound and important development in our nation's history.

It is precisely at this point that the Catholic Church's teachings on the relation between the individual and the group become revelant. For Catholic thought, while recognizing that there is always going to be some tension between man and society, refuses to admit that there is any necessary opposition between the development of the individual and the welfare of the group. Quite the contrary; the Catholic position has always been that the development of the human personality depends to a large extent on the degree to which the individual is an intelligently integrated member of a group. There is no question but that the group exists for the good of the persons who make it up. The interests of the members of the group are best served when they freely cooperate for the good of the whole. The ultimate reason for this paradox is that man has been created a social animal and achieves his goals not as an isolated and lonely individualist but rather as a participating member of society. An organization which believes itself to be the Mystical Body of Christ, which demands membership in itself as a condition for salvation, and which offers as its supreme act of worship a community sacrifice, can hardly regard the passing of exaggerated individualism as an unmitigated evil.

Hence the Catholic Church is sympathetic to modern man's quest for community; but its idea of community is considerably different from the narrow, self-contained little world of the modern conformist, who goes along with the group to get away from problems which seem too big for him to face. Family life should not remove man from political and economic society, but instead should better equip him to go out into the world and face its complexities and contradictions. The local church is to be not so much a place where he will find tranquility and solace amid the confusions of life, as a place where he will obtain the spiritual strength he needs to transform the institutions in which men must live and work and try to save their souls. The neighborhood community (even if it is a suburb) is not an escape from the horrors of industrialism, but a center for the eventual reconquest and humanization of the city. The lay apostle, then, normally gets his formation and strength not only from isolated prayer and meditation but also from intelligent participation in a group. The purpose of the group is not to rein in the creativity of the individual but to spur it on.

Nor is Catholic thought necessarily opposed to the yearning for security which seems so typical of modern youth. Pope Pius XI, echoing St. Thomas Aquinas, has said that a certain modest share of this world's goods is not only not an obstacle to salvation, but is a distinct help. One wonders whether all the vocal opponents of "security" are seriously advocating insecurity, and whether they themselves are ready to forego their pension rights. One can no more abrogate the human longing for economic security than one can repeal the law of human nature. As Father Dennis Geaney, O.S.A., has pointed out, if people do not feel relatively secure, most of them are not going to feel they have any time to devote to the work of the apostolate.

To say that Catholic thinking is in sympathy with the search for community is not to say that Catholics should go along with everything which is masquerading under the name of community in our culture. The quest for community is still uncertain and probing. Many mistakes, some of them foolish, are bound to be made. Thinkometers, leaderless groups, personality tests, life-adjustment courses, brainstorming, and uniformly colored bathrobes are absurdities which merely manifest how far the search for community has yet to go. One of the major advantages of a free society like our own is that the trenchant criticism of a David Riesman or a William H. Whyte sets up counter-trends which help to purify the search for community from some of its more obvious mistakes. As a result of such criticism, it is now fashionable to be a bit of a non-conformist. In fact, if one really wishes to conform, one had better be something of a non-conformist, because nowadays everyone else is, or at least claims to be (to the immense delight of the salesmen of foreign automobiles) .

How can we distinguish community from conformity? How can we tell whether a given group is promoting creativity or destroying it? How can we separate Christian social-mindedness from oppressive groupism? In practice such distinctions are not always easy to make. But a good rule of thumb would be this: if membership in a group draws a person into facing the problems which exist in the world beyond the group and into trying to do something about these problems, then the group has the beginnings at least of true community. If, on the other hand, the group draws the attention of its members more and more within its own limits, then conformity is corrupting community. For the man whose interests and vision are widening is becoming more human, and the man whose interests and vision are narrowing is becoming less human. Where there is complacency and self-satisfaction there can be no real human community. Complacency, then, distinguishes conformity from community and is the enemy which must be fought if the American dream is not to end in a collectivist nightmare.

13
The Waning
of Enthusiasm

Enthusiasm is a good word, and the quality it represents is a good quality. The absence of enthusiasm —in the sense of a zealous, driving dedication to a series of goals—is a sure sign of stagnation. It is for this reason that an observer of the American scene could be more than a little troubled by the waning of enthusiasm in our republic.

I do not intend to discuss the relationship between misdirected enthusiasm and constructive enthusiasm: to ask, for example, whether the danger of the former is the price that must be paid for the benefit of the latter. Nor do I wish to consider the thesis of Gerald Johnson that the disappearance of the "lunatic fringe" is a sign that the American experiment is running out of gas.[1] In a much more limited framework I wish merely to question whether in the educated middle-class version of Catholicism which is developing in this country there is much room for enthusiasm; I wish merely to ask if the newly dominant patterns of American Catholicism do not put considerable obstacles in the way of the development of authentic enthusiasts.

It is not a simple task to define the qualities of an enthusiast. Certainly he must be a man of *vision*. He should have some of that quality which St. Frances Cabrini displayed when she spoke of the world's being too small for her zeal. His sights must be set above his own immediate surroundings, and reveal to him a vast and confused but splendid world. He must be able to penetrate beneath the appearances of things, to cut through the clichés and truisms by which he is surrounded.

[1] *The Lunatic Fringe* (Philadelphia: Lippincott, 1957).

He must be sensitive to delicate and changing nuances and grasp clearly the importance of new factors. He should be able to see new relationships and see them quickly. In short, the enthusiast must have about him something of the visionary.

Closely connected to vision is *imagination*. The enthusiast must not only see things as they really are, he must also be able to see them the way they should be and—this is crucial—the way they *can* be. His mind must be agile in creating new plans and even, if necessary, new worlds.

He realizes, of course, that imagination is no substitute for thought, but he also perceives that thought without imagination must often remain unproductive. His approach is always flexible, and he is intrigued by novelties and gimmicks, though he must always be careful not to be carried away by them. No matter how old he is, he has never lost his youthful wonder.

Vision and imagination, however, are not enough unless the potential enthusiast is *restless*. He must be dissatisfied with things as they are and have a burning desire to change them. He can never be complacent, never think that his task is finished, or that his techniques have become perfect, or that his answers are definitive.

He may not believe in the inevitability of progress, but he knows that progress will never occur if he begins to relax. He must want to stir people up, to enkindle in them some of the flame that he feels within himself. He has come to cast fire on the earth.

As an almost inevitable consequence of this restlessness comes *a willingness to take chances,* to stake much on a single throw of the dice. He cannot be a reckless gambler, for recklessness will hurt his cause. He must shrewdly and carefully weigh alternatives, but he realizes too that much human action can be based upon probabilities and that even the best-made plans must often be tossed out the window.

A conservative refusal to run any risk of failure would mean immobilism; and a stubborn clinging to outmoded techniques would mean an empty formalism. Neither of these can the true enthusiast abide.

In this description of the enthusiast no mention has been made of the object of his energies. He may be enthusiastic about the climbing of Everest, the discovery of a polio vaccine, the building of a ballistic missile.

If one were to apply these four qualities, however, to the spreading of the kingdom of Christ, the enthusiastic Christian would be one who sees clearly the full implications of the redemption and the Mystical Body, who has the imagination to grasp ways whereby this Good News must be spread in his own time, who is consumed by a gnawing restlessness to see that the Good News is preached to and accepted by all men, and who possesses the courage to depart from the ordinary routine of life to do his work for Christ.

The enthusiastic Christian and the zealous apostle, in other words, are one and the same person. (One would presume that it is not necessary to list the obvious dangers of enthusiasm. It is not always easy to distinguish the prophet from the fanatic, the genius from the madman. Unfortunately, a safe judgment about an enthusiast can be made in most cases only after he is dead.)

If one considers the emergent Catholic middle class, one can find little inclination to enthusiasm of the religious variety—or of any other variety, for that matter. To say this is not necessarily to criticize individuals or denigrate a class. If a newly educated Catholic population is lacking in enthusiasm, it is not the result of laziness or malice but rather that of being part of mid-twentieth century American culture.

From the new Catholic middle class one can reasonably expect a very high level of observable religious practice (perhaps the highest of a large group in the history of the Church), but one will obtain dedicated enthusiasm only after the overcoming of considerable obstacles.

When all is said, however, the fact remains that enthusiasm of any kind is rapidly vanishing from the American scene. Optimism and enthusiasm of the Walt Whitman or Teddy Roosevelt type may still be part of our official creed, but few Americans give these dogmas much more than lip service. The rugged individualist of the frontier has about the same relationship to modern Americans as Achilles did to fourth-century Greeks.

The studies of Riesman and Whyte to which we have already referred merely confirm what many people had already guessed: *Homo Americanus* at mid-century is a very careful and conservative sort of fellow. The reasons for this change are many—four wars (three hot, one cold) in thirty-five years, the severe jolt of the Great Depression and the reverse jolt of the Great Boom, the always present threat of the Big Explosion. But whatever the cause, the enthusiast is vanishing from the American scene. Riesman's "inside dopester" seems to be taking his place.

Insofar as the Catholic population is very rapidly being assimilated into the mainstream of American life, the Catholic enthusiast is vanishing too—if indeed he was ever very much in evidence. It is instructive to analyze the reasons for his disappearance.

The middle-class *world vision*, even though it may be profound in its own way, is severely limited. In mid-century America it is primarily a domestic vision. As Riesman says of a group he studied:

The demands these men were willing to put both on themselves and their planet were, I thought, rather modest: they expected to have a good professional or corporate job, pay around $15,000, enough (as they figured it) to pay for a wife, three or four children, a home in the suburbs, a boat on a lake, two cars, and cultural amenities. The family—actual or prospective—loomed large in their thinking: . . . society small; their own careers were somewhere in between.[2]

Mutatis mutandis, this gray flannel goal is fast becoming typical of American society, if it is not so already. Middle-class man's vision is: home, family, local neighborhood, job, and the trip back and forth to the job. (In the case of middle-class woman the last two, and sometimes the last three, can be omitted.) By almost any standard but his own, his goals are immense, but he realizes that it is part of his American heritage that he will be able to achieve them with careful planning and hard work. He sees no reason to get excited.

In this vision there is little room for *imagination.* Are there millions starving in India? That's a shame, but India is a long way off, and if the Indians weren't so friendly to the Russians they might not have so much trouble. Is there a serious race problem in his city? He thinks all men should have equal rights, but there is not much he can do about it unless some member of a minority group should move into his neighborhood. Are politics corrupt? So long as the street in front of his house and the school his children attend are in reasonable repair, he doesn't see what good his one vote will do.

2 "The Suburban Sadness," in *The Suburban Community,* ed. William M. Dobriner (New York: Putnam, 1958).

Are there migrant workers, sub-proletarians who do not share in the American dream? How can he be expected to do anything for them? Is the neo-pagan Western world hungering to hear the message of Christ with something of its pristine vigor? Well, he goes to church every Sunday, doesn't practice birth control, and is giving his family a Catholic education. Does Jesus demand generosity from the members of His Mystical Body? Our friend is a generous contributor to regular and special collections. He is too busy to give these problems much thought; the little reading he forces upon himself offers only meager stimulation.

There may be a considerable amount of anxiety in his life, but there is little in the way of prophetic *restlessness*. One may be permitted to wonder if it is possible to be a prophet on a stomach which is almost always full. The standard of living of most Americans is so high that there is really very little left to get restless about. The basic needs of almost all Americans, the minimum comforts of most, and the maximum comforts of many, are already being satisfied or are at least within the economy's power to satisfy.

There may be many unfulfilled needs in our own schools, highways, recreational facilities and in under-developed countries, but these things are normally beyond the vision of middle-class man.

To quote Riesman for the last time: "We are a generation, prepared for Paradise Lost, who do not know what to do with Paradise Found."[3]

Nor, one might add, are we very much concerned about spreading Paradise to others less fortunate than ourselves.

Of course, spiritual restlessness can coexist with material abundance, but it does not seem to very often. The member of the Catholic middle class

[3] *Op. cit.*

thinks of himself as a good Catholic (and by most of the standards held up to him he is), but hardly as a missionary. If he is told that he cannot be a good Catholic unless he is a missionary, he is puzzled. Missions are for the Maryknollers and other such groups; of course, he will generously contribute financial support to their work.

Prophets were people who lived in the Old Testament, and apostles were the men who founded the Church. They were great men, but they did not have a job to hold down or a family to support. And those Catholic laity who are receiving some acclaim as lay apostles cannot find the time for such work unless they are cheating on their job or their family. There are just so many hours in the day.

Finally, middle-class man is not given to *taking chances.* The scientists that work for him have mastered most of the forces of nature. Plague, famine, drought are no longer threats. His life is relatively independent of the vagaries of nature and with each passing year becomes more so. He is therefore strongly tempted to feel that there are few things in his life he cannot control; if he is spared illness, sudden death, a major war or a major depression, he feels that it is within his power to meet all of life's contingencies. His life is reduced to a series of mathematical formulae arrived at by the use of the slide rule and actuarial tables. I know of teen-agers who choose their future occupations with a view to the cost of sending their unborn children to college (and often the colleges are already selected).

In this kind of existence there is little room for the taking of any but the most carefully calculated of risks. Occupational success is the measure of a man's worth (just as "successful" children are the measure of a woman's worth), and this can be achieved only by rigorous planning and conscientious work. There is no time for things that deviate from The Plan or might even upset it completely. Too much is at stake. Within the limits set up by The Plan, the middle-class Catholic will be only too happy to help his church; but this is distinctly a secondary vocation.

If the Holy Spirit wishes to generate enthusiasm among the Catholic middle class in this country, He must penetrate through several layers of cultural obstacles before He can touch hearts. That hearts are still touched does not prove the absence of obstacles but merely the power of the Spirit.

There are certain implications in the waning of enthusiasm for the liturgical and apostolic movements in this country. The increased popularity of liturgical participation and the rapid spread of the Catholic Action movements (particularly CFM) have been hailed as signs of great progress. And indeed they are. However, we must not be deceived as to the nature of this progress.

The flourishing new movements are the result of enthusiasm and the possible seed bed of more enthusiasm; but this does not mean that all or even most of the people involved are enthusiasts in any but the most remote sense of the word. They are rather good Catholics who look on the movements as splendid organizations, but hardly as training grounds for enthusiastic lay apostleship.

There are, of course, a number of enthusiasts in these movements, but it is at least open to question whether they are enthusiastic because they are in the movements or joined the movements because they were enthusiastic. The family movements in particular are faced with the difficult task of breaking the confining bonds of what most Americans consider family problems.

That the doctrines of the apostolic and liturgical movements have become reasonably popular and widespread is certainly a cause for rejoicing; but we must not assume that they have penetrated very deeply.

Few people would have supposed even five years ago that explicit summaries of *Rerum Novarum, Quadragesimo Anno* and *Mediator Dei* would so soon find their way into grammar school textbooks. But all too often words have passed from the mouths of the prophets (such as Msgr. Ryan or Dom Virgil) into the pages of a textbook without ever finding their place in the hearts of the average Catholic.

The cultural barriers to enthusiasm can be broken down, but it is by no means an easy task. For what is involved is the changing of basic attitudes and the decompartmentalization of life. Further, recent studies of college students indicate that the changing of an attitude is a far more difficult task than most people had thought.[4] In fact, the surveys in question indicate that a college education very rarely produces a significant change in affective orientations. I have been told that these surveys were so damaging to the philosophy of American education that attempts were made to suppress them.

But while they may embarrass the secular educator, they offer very little consolation to those of us who at one time expected the observe-judge-act technique of certain Catholic movements to produce great and rapid results.

There are at least three avenues of investigation which might prove useful in the campaign to change unenthusiastic attitudes.

The first would be to encourage attempts toward an intellectual revival among the middle class. It should be obvious by now that intellectualism and education do not go hand in hand. However, the serious pursuit of a yet obscure truth can generate

[4] Cf. Philip E. Jacob, *Changing Values in College* (New York: Harper, 1958).

both restlessness and vision. Hence, efforts like that of Fr. Rooney's Catholic Commission on Intellectual and Cultural Affairs to promote an environment of respect for learning are most important if enthusiasm is to be reborn (though indeed these efforts have value in themselves and must not be looked on merely as means to other ends).

Secondly, one can, it seems, expect great things from the limited-service lay mission groups such as the Association for International Development. It is possible and even likely that such groups can harness the enthusiasm of youth before it is stifled by the routine of occupational or domestic life. It would be reasonable to suppose that after two or three years on the mission a lay person would not sink into apostolic lethargy.

Thirdly, we must not underestimate the influence of men and women who are already in the grip of enthusiasm. The college surveys mentioned above indicate that when an attitudinal change does occur it is most often the result of the influence of an extraordinary teacher. Who can calculate, for example, the influence of a Dom Virgil or a Msgr. Ryan or a Msgr. Hillenbrand or a Dorothy Day?

This leaves us, however, with one last interesting and crucial question: Who will bring enthusiasm to those of us who by profession are bound to be enthusiasts? Who will bring savor to the salt, who will prophesy to the prophets?

14
Beat, Cool—
and Lonely

Americans seem to have an incurable tendency to label historical epochs. We've had our Gay Nineties, our Roaring Twenties, our Lost Generation. The extreme self-consciousness that modern social science has introduced into our culture has recently added a new twist to this name-giving proclivity. We try not to put a label on our own times, to classify the present before it can become the past. Hence we are told that now we are in the midst of the Age of Conformity or the Indifferent Generation or the Beat Generation or the Silent Generation. It is, of course, extremely dangerous to try to write history before it has happened, but if we try to find a common note running through these analyses of our time we must say that, just as the time after World War I was the Age of Disillusionment, so the time after World War II could well be called the Age of Disengagement.

As Romano Guardini has pointed out, the modern world with all its calm Cartesian certainties has come to an end. The picture of harmony between man, science, and nature went up in the smoke of the ovens of Dachau and vanished forever in the mushroom cloud over Hiroshima. The rational universe has been destroyed, the dream of progress has turned into a nightmare, the alienation of man from nature, from his fellows and himself is complete. The walls of the secular-humanist city are crumbling and the hordes of New Barbarians are waiting outside the gates.

Such a picture may well be too pessimistic. Guardini may be too much influenced by the conditions in postwar Germany before the present German economic boom began. However, a great number of people feel, though perhaps only subconsciously, that the picture is not completely inaccurate. The modern world seems to be a mad mechanized monster heading blindly for its doom, and there is nothing which can be done to stop it. The forces let loose in the last four centuries have gotten out of control and are going to destroy the world they have created. So it is the wise man who disengages himself from this absurdity, who escapes involvement in this madness. The only way to survival is to face the meaninglessness of our lives and courageously accept our own doom.

Thus speak the European Existentialists and thus speak also their American imitators, the Beat, the Hipsters. They are by their own admission "hip without being slick, intelligent without being corny, know all about Pound without being pretentious, they are very quiet, they are very Christlike." (They are *not*, by the way.) They have stepped off the trolley in the conviction that there is no place to go. They believe no longer in goodness or progress; they have given up all desire to control nature, events or people so that they can "flow with the real tides of existence, those which flow beyond guilt, hate or love." Not for them the life of the Square, with his suburban picture window looking out over a graveyard. They have "cut out" (divorced themselves from society), so that they can "get with it" ("to set out on that uncharted journey into the rebellious imperatives of the self"). They went no more of other people's habits, other people's defeats, boredom and quiet frustration. So they escape to their Bohemias in San Francisco (with imitations throughout the country), where they can at all times be cool — sophisticatedly non-involved. The crowning irony is that the Squares won't leave them alone, but crowd into their hideouts to gawk. (This does not seem to bother the Beat as much as it might, because this means that the Squares will buy Beat novels and poems and pay for them with good old-fashioned Square money.)

It is not for us to say in this chapter whether the Beatniks have any real literary merit or whether the world of Kerouac and Ginsberg, of Brando and Dean is not merely a world of little children who have never grown up. From a sociological viewpoint the emergence of the Beat—and their inevitable imitators, the pseudo-beat—is a significant sign of the times.

What has occurred to few people (and least of all to the Beat) is that the new Bohemians are not the only ones who are running away from modern civilization. Just about everyone is. Even the Squares are running; in fact, one might even say that especially the Squares are running.

As sociologists and psychologists study more carefully the suburban migration, many of them are beginning to believe that the movement to Suburbia is, in part at least, a flight from the ugliness and confusion of modern industrialism. As we have noted, the mere presence of vacant land on the edge of a city is not of itself an explanation for suburban sprawl when apartment dwellings in the central city could have been much more convenient. Suburbia vaguely represents the refined, peaceful leisure which the old aristocracy had at their country estates. Suburbia offers modern man a chance to "get away from it all," and there's nothing he wants more. The suburban vision involves enjoying the fruits of industrialism without paying the prices it so far has demanded. The Square wants to be "cool" too, and his air-conditioned suburban home promises to be cool indeed.

The political, social and economic orders seem to be twisted and frightening messes. All the old primary groups—the groups where face-to-face, personal contact existed—either have been destroyed or are being destroyed. Modern man looks at these orders and throws up his hands in horror and disgust. He wants no part of them unless it is forced on him. He will make that commitment to them which is necessary for his survival, but he will get out as quickly as he can. He flees to his family and his religion, for in the orders of domesticity and faith some comforting primary relationships still remain. Like the Beat, he is seeking some new kind of community where he can undo the effects of his triple alienation. In Suburbia he sees a place where he can get back into contact with nature (his lawn and barbecue pit), his fellow men (the family), and himself. If he is "other-directed," it is because in our senseless world there is no way to get direction but from others. If he is a conformist, it is because he desperately wants that community which industrialism has destroyed. If he does not want to get "involved," it is because he fears that involvement will destroy the precious crumbs of happiness that he has managed to scrape together.

How many priests engaged in the lay apostolate have seen people hold back a commitment to apostolic activity precisely because they were afraid of "becoming too involved"? How many times have they heard the words, "I'll be glad to help, but if I took charge I'd get too involved"? Disengagement from difficult tasks, non-involvement in tangled problems— this is the way to interior peace, this is the way out of the frightening complications of modern life. Hence we should not be surprised that every study of college students shows that they list as their goals, first, happy family life, then business or professional success (a poor second), and finally service to mankind (an even poorer third). They, as well as the denizens of San Francisco, plan to be cool, so they can cut out— at least as much as is compatible with enjoying the conveniences that the hated big city is producing.

Unfortunately for both the Beat and the Square, their vision is doomed to be destroyed. Even if one wants to, one cannot "cut out." The modern world continues its relentless pursuit, whether it be with gawking tourists in "The Place" or urban blight spreading to the suburbs almost as soon as they are built. One cannot abdicate from the human race. Non-involvement is out of the question, disengagement is impossible. To be human is to be caught in the necessity of being committed, of being *engaged*. One cannot escape from the modern world any more than one can escape from being human.

The more sophisticated critics of our society are beginning to recognize this fact. Erich Fromm attributes neurosis not so much to non-fulfillment of recognized needs as to the ignoring of the needs for creativity, service, and significance. He claims that much of our modern unhappiness comes from the fact that we feel we are losing opportunities but are not sure of what the opportunities are. David Riesman speaks of the "suburban sadness" which results when the owners of the Good Life find that it is not nearly as rewarding as it promised to be, that, in fact, it seems to be curiously empty. Russell Lynes asks the impudent question, "Were we not better off when we had a depression and were linked to our fellow men at least by our common suffering?" Despite the Beat and the Square, commitment seems necessary for happy human living.

What form must such a commitment take? For the Catholic there are two broad choices: the religious life (including the clerical state) and the lay apostolate. Thus, to put the matter quite bluntly, a Catholic lay person in the twentieth century must have some sort of apostolic commitment if he is to have a full and happy life. If he does not make this commitment, he will become a victim either of Erich Fromm's "guilt" or David Riesman's "suburban sadness." When he rejects apostolic commitment for fear of becoming "too involved," the layman is throwing away a precious chance for happiness. For in the lay state the normal way of contact with the Almighty must be through action in the temporal order. To condemn this order because it is profane, or to fear it because it is confused or dangerous, is not only unchristian, not only foreign to the mind of all the recent popes, it is also exceedingly foolish. It means a tragic waste.

This does not mean that the Catholic suburbanite will not be happy unless he is helping in the acculturation of the Negro groups that are moving into the center of the metropolis he has deserted. But it does mean that if the suburbanite is not engaged in this or some similar apostolic commitment he is going to be considerably less happy than he could be or should be; for he will have passed up an opportunity to draw closer to the Source of all happiness.

Let us avoid all oversimplification. The apostolate is not a substitute for tranquilizers or shock therapy. One does not get over one's anxiety merely by joining a Catholic Action group. On the contrary, the apostolate requires the most steady of nerves. Apostolic involvement does not promise peace, but it does promise happiness, which is quite another thing.

Nor is a commitment to the apostolate as easy as it might sound on paper. For the Beat and the Square are right; the world is chaotic and frightening; the temporal order is being torn by technological and social forces which are not out of control. Modern civilization is rent by dirty, messy problems to which there seem to be no solutions. The aim of the Christian is to restore order, to reintegrate all things in Christ. But this reintegration will take many generations. The day is long since past when we could talk glibly about a "new synthesis" as though it were just around the corner. Naturally speaking, the work of the apostolate seems hopeless; the obstacles are so great, the means so puny. We have no reason on natural grounds to expect success. Even moderate success seems to be unlikely in the lives of any of us. The only thing we have any right to look forward to in our collapsing modern world is defeat, discouragement, and frustration. We trust that the future will be brighter than this, but we realize that, if it is, the work of the Holy Spirit will have to be spectacular indeed (as it has been many times in the past).

Commitment to the apostolate, the kind of total commitment that precludes ever turning back, requires at least as much faith and courage as the existentialist commitment of the Beat. It involves accepting meaninglessness and absurdity, it means facing irrationality and chaos. But it means more; it means believing that beneath the irrationality there is at work a Reason, that in the midst of the disorder there is a Plan and an Order. It is far easier to resign oneself to an irrationality which one perceives than to work for the fulfillment of a Plan which one does not see or understand. It takes far more heroism to be a Christian than to be an existentialist.

Yet once the commitment is made, there does come a certain serenity, if not peace; the serenity of those who believe that they, like Apollo and Paul, are planting and watering, and that God will some day most certainly grant the increase.

15
Permanent
Prosperity?

Whenever thoughtful Catholics get together, there is a certain pattern that their discussions are likely to follow. They will talk about the training of lay leaders, the expansion of the Catholic Action movements, the liturgical revival, the deepening of the intellectual life and similar problems. There is little chance that their conversation will turn to one of the most awesome aspects of post-war American living: our prosperity.

To a generation raised in the dark days of the Great Depression, the possibility of permanent prosperity does not seem to merit serious worry. Yet such a possibility, in itself so eminently desirable, has frightening implications and can bring a whole new complex of problems to the American Church.

To say that America is by and large a prosperous nation today is not to deny that there are soft spots or that social injustice still exists. Certainly the migrant workers, large groups of farmers, and many Spanish-speaking peoples are not enjoying prosperity. Housing leaves much to be desired. Negroes are not given the opportunities they should have. Education and health facilities are sadly deficient. Installment buying is out of hand. There are far too many working wives.

But, by and large, most Americans "never had it so good." Statistical proof of this happy situation is easy to advance. According to a survey made by the Department of Commerce, the average family income in 1955 was $5,520. There were almost eight million new automobiles sold in 1955. Housing construction, although far from adequate, is at record levels. Deepfreezes, electric dishwashers, air conditioners, and color TV sets are purchased as fast as they can be produced. The wardrobes in suburban homes are crowded with an incredibly wide variety of clothes. Thirty million dollars is spent each year on leisure pastimes. "Pie in the sky when you die" has become pie á la mode on earth—and both the pie and ice cream are taken out of the family deepfreeze. This is not a true picture of all Americans, but it is true of a greater number than ever before, and of a constantly increasing number.

"Will it last?" This is the important question. A good number of experts are beginning to say it might very well last. There may be jolts, temporary recessions (as in 1958-59), severe dislocations in certain sections of the economy. But, in the long run, a continuation of prosperity is much more likely than a massive depression of the variety of twenty years ago.

There are many reasons for this bright view of the future. The staggering rise in population, the countless industrial revolutions caused or promised by automation, atomic energy, electronics, climate control and sun power, the tremendous increase in capital outlays—all these are fair weather signs to the economist. Military spending seems likely to continue for the foreseeable future. Making guns and tanks, rockets and guided missiles appears to be filling the same purpose that Lord Keynes facetiously suggested the building of pyramids might have filled in the '30's— guaranteeing a demand sufficient to keep the economy going.

The built-in stabilizers of the New Deal reconstruction would certainly cushion a depression. Social security, unemployment insurance (and the guaranteed annual wage), graduated income taxes, and bank deposit insurance all co-operate, it is said, to insure that a recession shall not get out of hand quite so rapidly.

Finally, economists believe that no administration would dare permit a big depression. Practical politicians know that this would be political suicide. Our depression-fighting tools may be crude, but if World War II proved anything, it proved that the government can, by spending enough money, bring the country out of a depression.[1]

The experts who predict lasting prosperity may well be wrong; they have been in the past. But Catholics in America must be prepared to deal with the problems which will arise if these experts are right. One of the most interesting aspects of permanent prosperity—and one to which we give little serious thought—is the problem of leisure.

The problem is far different from the hoary objection that work weeks should not be shortened because people would just waste their time and an idle mind is the devil's workshop. But, as George Soule points out in his *Time for Living,* time is an important factor in the economy, just as are other factors like resources, labor and capital. Time is a commodity to be purchased, and it must be kept in balance with the other factors of production if the economy is to remain stable. Soule does not, therefore, consider the rise of a new leisure class a luxury. He thinks the exploding production curve makes it a necessity. For, if people do not have more time to consume the goods they are producing, then demand for the constant stream of new goods will slacken. Thus, a careful balance must be kept between time spent producing and time spent consuming. This "consumption time" is what we would call leisure, and it must be

[1] Whether we have the tools to fight inflation—depression's opposite number—is another question. Our country is conditioned to fear deflation and to demand stringent measures to combat it. The fear of inflation is not nearly so strong, except among certain relatively small groups. The real danger may be not depression but inflation—not runaway inflation, but rather the creeping variety.

constantly increasing if the economy is to remain stable.

If Soule is correct, Lord Keynes' revolution against the Puritan ethic has at last become complete. The ideal of long hours of diligent work and that thrifty hoarding of every penny has been destroyed. Today people are told that spending money is more important to the economy than saving, that consumption is rapidly becoming more important than production, and leisure almost as essential as work. The inner-directed Puritan is being replaced by the other-directed "consumption man."

We can view with mixed emotions the way in which this new leisure is being used. Certainly there is nothing to condemn in the "do it yourself" craze, the increased interest in music, the number of books read, the expansion of sports, travel and other forms of recreation. But when these things reach such massive scales, can good taste and balance be preserved?

For example, how much of the current hi-fi mania is motivated by a love for and an understanding of good music and how much is just a sophisticated desire for novelty? Both factors are involved, of course, but the exact proportion is hard to judge.

We must not fall into the error of those European critics who consider Americans to be cultural barbarians. On the other hand, certain of the manifestations of popular culture which are presented to us in TV, the cinemascope, and the billboard advertisements are enough to give us pause. "Rock and Roll" can coexist with Beethoven's *Ninth, Richard III* with Jackie Gleason. All have their proper place, but we have no guarantee that in a leisure culture they will be put in their proper place.

What will be done with this greatly increased time for leisure? What happens to the intellectual and spiritual life in an age of abundance and opulence? Will there not be a tendency for thought processes to atrophy? Will wealthy, pleasure-sated humans stop thinking? Will they even be able to think that they should get up and turn the TV off?

When the senses are filled with vivid images from every side, does the human animal dispense completely with his creative imagination? In the midst of plenty, does not prayer become extremely difficult, if not impossible? Does mortification have any meaning to people who have never known material want? Is there any room for God in an age of plenty? Is there a contradiction between a Cadillac and a St. Christopher medal? Can man, when he has so many things in this world, seriously long for the next?

There is another side to the coin. Is it possible to be happy with so many material goods? Does not a hoard of possessions simply cause greater desires? Is it not true that the more we have the more we will want? When luxuries become necessities, does not human nature hunt avariciously for newer and more enticing luxuries? Won't leisure time, consumption time, begin to pall upon us? Isn't there a danger that we might start longing for the "good old days" of the forty-hour week when we had useful and constructive things to do with our waking day?

We need not be too pessimistic in considering these questions. The evils indicated are not inevitable. But we would be deceiving ourselves if we did not admit that they are distinct possibilities.

Leisure of itself does not necessarily mean relaxation, and this brings up another and deeply paradoxical aspect of permanent prosperity. People have never had so much opportunity for leisure, yet they have never been so busy. They have no time to read, to pray, to go to church, to join apostolic movements; no time to spend with the children, to take a rest, to go on a vacation. Is the frantic activity anything more than an attempt to escape from the frustrations which prosperity seems to increase? Americans compulsively, restlessly rush through life. They seem to be haunted by a fear that there is something they will miss. With more available substitutes for the Absolute, our hungers for Him seem to be deeper.

We are almost afraid to slow down in our relentless pursuit of happiness for fear that if we stop to think we may make the alarming discovery that we are running very rapidly in the wrong direction. In a world of leisure and abundance the tasks of the Hound of Heaven may be much more difficult.

It would seem to follow that one of the most serious educational problems facing American Catholics is the spreading of good taste and the ability to budget time. These were virtues for which our ancestors had little need, but which may be essential to the spiritual development of our children. If we do not learn how to use prosperity, we may become its slaves. We must become convinced that material abundance solves no human problems even though it may furnish a framework in which problems can be faced with greater ease. If these lessons are not learned, it seems quite possible that the next generation will be a restless and frustrated one. A discontented poor man may join a revolution, but a discontented "rich" man may well start one.

Sociologists tell us that the fourth generation, which feels little of the social pressures to ascend the ladder of respectability, is the one which should be creative. Leisure classes have certainly contributed greatly to human culture in the past, but a leisure class is not automatically creative. There are many young people growing up in the suburbs today who scribble poetry or write short stories that show the beginnings of promise. But they are very secretive about their efforts, because their parents look upon such inclinations as being silly, if not dangerous. "Poets don't make money."

If we expect our leisure society to make significant

contributions to the human heritage, we may have a major task in working for a social climate where contributions other than advertising copy or cinematic soap opera scripts are encouraged.

There are no easy answers to the questions proposed in this chapter. In a world where poverty is still widespread, where hunger is a constant possibility for most people, where thermonuclear annihilation is an ever present threat, it seems almost sacrilegious to talk of the problems of prosperity and leisure. They are not the most serious problems facing American Catholics. And yet they are serious enough because they are recognized by so very few.

16
Leisure and
Popular Culture

Speaking of the "Middletown" of 1925 Robert Lynd observed that leisure was "becoming more passive, more formal, more organized, more mechanized, and more commercialized." Lynd had epitomized the theory of American leisure which was to hold complete sway until the end of World War II and continue to find many advocates in the decade and a half that followed. If American use of leisure was so bad, the migration to the suburbs would very likely make things worse. Since more leisure was one of the goals of the move to Suburbia, it followed that leisure pursuits would become criteria of social status. Leisure activity, already irrational and inhuman, would become compulsively so. The passivity, mechanization, and commercialization of leisure would prove to be just one more link in the chain of suburban tyranny.

To what extent have these dire predictions proven true? The answer to this question has touched off one of the "great debates" of contemporary sociology and social criticism. One side has marshalled considerable statistical evidence to prove that American popular culture is at an all-time low, while the other has gathered almost as much evidence to prove that this same popular culture is better than it ever was and constantly improving. After examining the evidence gathered by both sides one cannot help feeling that they both are right.

Anyone possessing the relatively unimpaired use of his five senses cannot doubt that, from one point of view, popular culture in our country is deteriorating every year. The various mass media have become shills trying to hold the attention of an audience while modern pitchmen display their wares. TV, once the scene of promising and interesting experimentation, has fallen under the sway of westerns, musical varieties, and, until recently, the big-time quiz shows. AM radio has become the domain of the sleek disk jockeys and their adolescent female admirers. The latter are a group which may have their charms, but are hardly qualified to dictate the musical tastes of the nation. The slick magazines serve up a diet of soulless short stories or gruesome pictures of starving Asiatics juxtaposed with cosmetic ads. *Confidential* sells two million copies an issue. Mike Hammer, with his thirty million paperbacks, is considerably better known than his more admirable grandfather, Sherlock Holmes. The hard-cover novelists have found that the only way they can compete with the paperback hacks (or eventually join them) is to furnish their readers with even more clinically detailed sexual "kicks." On the few occasions when Hollywood dabbles with something serious, its compulsive fear of offending anyone forces it back on either stock happy endings or equally stock unhappy endings.

Even the newspapers, which have not always had the highest standards, seem to be slipping. Few Dunnes or Menckens are around to poke fun at our national peculiarities; one searches in vain for a younger Walter Lippmann. The new molders of opinion are either strident columnists with the "inside story" or the mammoth "news magazines" which have developed distortion to an art of the greatest skill. One watches in horror as a great paper like the *New York Herald Tribune* tries to hold ground against its more sensational competitors.

Thus, in brief outline, do the pessimists state their case. While one might disagree with the details or feel that the description is somewhat exaggerated, it is difficult to disagree with its general conclusions. The pessimists, however, are not content with merely describing the general low estate of American popular culture. They have worked out a theory to explain the inevitability of this situation. According to the theory, folk culture died with the coming of industrialism. Mass culture is a commercialized corruption of high culture manufactured by the technicians of the mass media to sate the leisure appetites of the urbanized, industrialized masses. This *kitsch* (as the Germans call popular culture) is bound to be synthetic. To sell, it must appeal to a large audience; to appeal to a large audience, it must find the lowest common denominator of that audience. As a result we have a kind of Gresham's law of popular culture: the bad drives the good out of circulation. For mass culture feeds on high culture as a worm feeds on a leaf. It may bring to the masses some of the products of high culture, but only after having reduced them to a tasteless, colorless homogeneity. In short, an artist cannot produce good material for a mass audience. If one wishes to consume mass culture, one must get rid of individual tastes. For in mass society there is no room for individual differences; nor can there be.

The optimists admit that there is a considerable amount of truth in the criticism of their rivals, but claim that it is by no means the whole truth. In the field of books, for example, not all of the 8,000,000 paperbacks sold last year were gobbled up by the sex-and-gore trade. In recent years, the *Iliad* has sold 500,000 copies and the *Odyssey* 800,000. *Wuthering Heights* has passed the million mark and Jane Austen's *Pride and Prejudice* has nearly the same total. One edition of Dante's *Inferno* has sold more than a quarter of a million, and books by such varied authors as Plato, Whitehead, and Toynbee are selling in the six-figure bracket. Quality paperbacks are proving quite profitable; David Riesman's *The Lonely*

Crowd, of all books, has sold over a quarter of a million copies, and its brothers in social criticism, *The Organization Man* and *The Hidden Persuaders,* seem destined to do equally well.

Nor are American musical tastes beyond redemption. There are 200 symphony orchestras in the country. Not only do twice as many people go to classical musical events as went in 1940, but almost three times as many (around 40,000,000) attend such concerts as go to baseball games. Some 30,000,000 classical records are sold each year. Twenty million recordings of Arturo Toscanini have been purchased since 1920 and some 60,000,000 records of the works of Mozart. A few years ago, Wanda Ladowska's harpsichord recording of the Goldberg Variations sold 20,000 sets within three months.

Even TV has its moments, such as the by now almost legendary showing of the Olivier production of *Richard III.* Much less spectacular, but much more important in the long run, are the 400 hours of programming by almost 30 educational stations with a potential audience of 50,000,000. Radio is not beyond redemption, as the 15,000,000 loyal listeners of the Metropolitan Opera broadcasts prove.

The optimists are in no position to deny that much of American popular culture is almost unbearably bad. But they think the evidence proves that it is not necessarily that way. The argument that mass production destroys individual tastes does not seem to hold true in a society as large as ours where a considerable number of individuals with unusual tastes can make all sorts of exotic cultural products commercially profitable. For example, as I type these lines I could turn on my mass-produced FM set and listen to a mass-produced recording of Beniamino Gigli singing *Arie Antiche.* It seems most unlikely that, if I were a devotee of seventeenth-century songs, I wouldn't mind too much the fact that mass productions made it pos-

sible for several thousand other people to enjoy Beniamino at the same time I did. In fact, if it were not for
mass production, very few of the admirers of *Arie
Antiche* would ever have a chance to hear them. To
maintain that mass enjoyment of a work of art either
cheapens the work or cheapens the enjoyment is to
come dangerously close to snobbery.

There are, then, two counter-trends in American
popular culture, one going up and the other going
down. Apparently in our rich and varied society the
two can coexist. For a study of the suburbs the important question is which trend seems dominant in
Suburbia. As bad as some of the aspects of the suburban leisure situation might appear, there is some evidence (albeit minute) that the positive elements in
popular culture are stronger in Suburbia than elsewhere.

First of all, suburbanites are more given to active
than to passive recreation. Golf, bridge, gardening,
boating, "do it yourself," swimming, tennis—all are
extremely popular. As we noted elsewhere, suburbanites much prefer to do things with others than by
themselves. So group recreation is replacing the lonely
spectatorism of decades gone by. Husbands and
wives spend their time together, and suburban communities abound with all kinds of social activities for
couples or families. William Whyte describes the
Park Forest community building with eight meetings
going on during a typical evening. One of the meetings, perhaps the most typical, was a meeting to form
another organization which would then proceed to
have its own meetings. Any suburbanite pastor or
curate will testify that Park Forest, in this respect at
least, is not unusual.

Whether all this group activity is good or bad has
been discussed in a previous chapter. Whether it is
an improvement in the use of leisure might be prob-
lematic. Much of it seems a trifle forced and frantic,

like the bright but brittle gaiety of suburban cock-
tail parties. For a deadly serious people, leisure can
be a deadly serious business. Not a little of the bustle of suburban social life looks aimless. One wonders
if people have to work as hard as that to have a good
time. Leisure can even turn into a burden. We must
enjoy ourselves whether we want to or not. Actually
the old dichotomy between passive and individual
leisure on the one hand and active and group
leisure on the other has lost much of its meaning. It
might be wondered which is more human—to listen
to a Mozart concerto by oneself or frantically to pur-
sue a golf ball with three men with whom one is competing for business success every other day of the
week. (Lest I make enemies of all my golf-playing
friends, let me stress that both can be constructive
uses of leisure.)

A more encouraging sign can be found in what
Russell Lynes call the increase in dilettantes.[1] For
Lynes the word is not to be used in the pejorative
sense. A dilettante is an amateur who has acquired
some of the competence of the professional. In whatever field he is interested—hi-fi, sports cars, jazz, the
dances of Tibet, or the jewelry of pre-Columbian
Mexico—he demands high quality. In the pursuit
of his particular interest he wants the very best and
often manages to find it. The suburban dilettante is
seeking quality for its own sake; he has, in part at
least, abandoned the old Puritan ideal that recreation
time must somehow or other be devoted to self-im-
provement—which normally meant economic self- improvement. Of course, the quality that the dilettante
seeks might be of little intrinsic value, but his approach to the good, the true and the beautiful is
closer to the ideal of Aristotle than is the crass utili-
tarianism of joining a country club "for business pur-

[1] "Time on Our Hands," *Harper's*, July, 1958, p. 36.

poses." It is just possible that good taste might be increasing in the suburbs.

How many of Lyne's dilettantes are there? Is there really a noticeable shift in leisure activities in Suburbia? There are not many statistical surveys to answer these questions, but the few that exist tend to tip the scales slightly in favor of the suburbanites. One University of Chicago study showed that there was a small but significant trend to higher "quality" leisure activities in the suburbs than in city neighborhoods *even in those city neighborhoods where people had the same income and occupation levels as in the suburbs.* If these statistics could be substantiated by later studies, it would indicate that the migration to Suburbia has meant a net improvement in the American use of leisure, even if such improvement be relatively small.

Actually, the debate as to whether suburban leisure is significantly more human than urban leisure is rather academic. If there has been a modern improvement in leisure activities in Suburbia, it merely serves to point up our national problem:

> Whichever way we turn or squirm, the fact keeps confronting us that America and Americans have available to them the resources both of mind and matter to build and support the finest culture the world has ever known; that until now many of these resources have been spent in foolish and sometimes ugly ways; that the resources nevertheless keep growing, and the chance remains. How can we take advantage of this opportunity?

> Can such a society, under the most favorable material conditions the world has ever experienced, rise to the occasion and prove itself worthy? Can it provide for the continuous free play of opposing systems of values and tastes, within the framework of democratic forms? Can

it make room for an expansion of those spiritual, creative impulses in man which meaner conditions of life do not allow to come to the surface? Can it find place in its halls of fame for men of letters and arts and science and ideas, as well as those of commerce and power and arms?[2]

These questions are of decisive importance. Industrialism has made greater leisure possible. Suburbia is an attempt to enjoy this leisure, an attempt by a larger number of people than was ever dreamed possible in the past history of the human race. The use of leisure may determine the ultimate fate of the suburbanite experiment. The acquiring of national good taste may be one of the most serious of our problems. Even though the battle for the right use of leisure might not be fought entirely in Suburbia, the suburbanites are undoubtedly among those who will have to join it. We can be sure that the battle is being won when more and more suburbanites become interested in those three all-important leisure activities described by Aristotle—poetry, politics, and philosophy.

[2] Melvin Tumin "Popular Culture and the Open Society," *Mass Culture* (Chicago: Free Press), p. 532.

17
Program for Oblivion

The *Harvard Business Review* is not considered in most circles to be a notably radical journal. Yet in a recent issue its quiet pages contain an article which may have effects as revolutionary as the Communist Manifesto and which could spell the beginning of the end of the suburban dream. The article "Management in the 1980's" by Harold J. Leavitt and Thomas L. Whisler, predicts the virtual end of Middle Management. If the authors are correct, the organization man will be dead by 1980, replaced by the far more efficient and far less neurotic digital computer. Any similarity between their sober vision and the far more dramatic *1984* of George Orwell is based on solid reality.

Suburbia is largely the result of the growth of middle management. It is inhabited by the countless assistant managers, junior executives, senior executives and assistant vice presidents who form the line of communication between the policy makers of large corporations (and unions and governments and universities) and the actual production of goods and services. Modern society is so complicated and the modern corporation so vast, that top management must rely on the lower ranks both for the information to make decisions and for co-operation to carry them out. Hence middle management has real, though limited, authority and real, though limited, decision-making power. When they make the proper decisions often enough, the members of middle management have some hope and some promise of rising into the magic circle at the top.

If we are to believe the *Harvard Business Review,*

the day of middle management is fast waning. Mathematics and the fantastic electronic computers are going to "program" the men of middle management out of business. Their tasks will in the next quarter of a century become just as routine as those of the laborer on the assembly line. Their decisions will no longer be based on human judgment but on simple routines ("programs") devised by Operations Research men. Worse still, they may not even be given the opportunity to follow established routines. They may simply implement decisions made for them by agile mechanical computers. Machines are already scheduling weekly production in some industries; the men who used to make up the schedules merely feed information in and receive the presumably infallible answer back. As the authors remark, the ability of the computers is improving every year; in the not too distant future the annual world chess championship will be a battle between two electronic brains.

What kind of change will this revolution in "information technology" make in our society? First of all, the men on top will be in much more effective control of operations. Decentralization of industry and participative management, made necessary by the complications of the first half of the twentieth century, will be reversed, and "recentralization" will set in. The power élite will have much more power. The authors of "Management in the 1980's" think that our society might begin to resemble some of the less progressive European nations—a tightly organized feudalism on top and a mass of technicians—white-collar and blue-collar—on the bottom. Some of the middle managers will disappear; some—those who know how to work out the "programs" and service the computers—will move into the top; the rest will become mere technicians. Just as the machine removed the need for the individual worker to use his judgment, so the computer removes the need for the manager to use his. It is just possible that the middle managers may not like this. Whether we can expect a re-enactment of the machine-smashing riots of the early nineteenth century is not certain; but Messrs. Leavitt and Whisler conservatively guess that "major resistances should be expected in the process of converting relatively autonomous and unprogrammed middle-management jobs to highly routinized programs."

Nor will the condition of top management be a bed of roses. The inertia of a middle-management bureaucracy might prevent good decisions made on the top from having their optimum effect, but it also prevented the bad decisions from bringing on immediate disaster. A large corporation could struggle along for some time with less than the most competent people in power. But "information technology" changes all that. The screen of middle management will be gone. The decisions of top management will bring success or disaster almost instantaneously. Hence the men at the top must have extraordinary ability. For, no matter how efficient the machines, someone (or more likely a group of someones) will have to decide in what directions the company should go and what questions the machines should be asked. These "programmers, creators, and committors" will have to be extremely "creative" people and will probably live in a world much like the world of advertising and similar "creative" professions today. The rat race will continue but only for the privileged few.

There are, according to the authors, two significant psychological implications for the largely suburbanite members and future members of middle management. They will not, in the first place, have jobs that are any more inherently significant than the role of knob twister on the assembly line. Whatever human satisfactions they are to have will necessarily come from off-the-job activities. Secondly, there will be practically no hope for them to move beyond the technician level. For the skills they will need to perform their daily task will be vastly different from the ones used by the "creative" group on top. Entrance into this top group will be from outside the corporation, the result of special training programs for exceptionally gifted young people. Apparently one need not think of arriving at a decision-making position without a Ph.D. in mathematics. Or, if the need for a few highly imaginative and creative individuals is made blindingly clear by the efficiency of the machines, philosophers and poets may yet be kings.

The world of Messrs. Leavitt and Whisler may never materialize.[1] The computers might not be quite as efficient replacements for human judgmental processes as they predict; but it would not be a particularly safe bet to say that their predictions will be very wrong. The implications for the suburban world sketchily described in this book are rather frightening. There seem to be two possibilities, neither pleasant. The first is that the escape from industrialism will become complete, that the suburban technicians will leave the big world of business in the hands of the "creative" minority on top and retreat into the bliss of suburban domesticity. The job will be an unpleasant few hours of the day necessary to provide the financial resources for the fun and games of suburban leisure. Interest in the world beyond the suburban boundaries, even now declining,

[1] "An even more horrifying view of the future can be found in the recent *Cybernation: The Silent Conquest*, Donald N. Michael. The Fund for the Republic, 1962. However, I am a little bit more skeptical about the predictions of Leavitt and Whisler than when I originally wrote this essay. Having had some experience with IBM machines in the last two years, I am not at all certain that they are going to replace mankind in the next 20 years. The problems discussed in this essay are real enough, but the Cybernetic apocalypse is not just around the corner."

will reach absolute zero. Suburban man will be contented and happy, and so thoroughly dehumanized that he won't even notice.

The other alternative seems more likely. Most Americans will not take kindly to the destruction of their success dream. The countless young executives who thought they were going to be "in" will find gradually that they have been left "out." The division between the "we" and the "they" will be much more sharply defined. Just as the worker found an answer to routinization with his union, so downgraded technicians of middle management can be expected to come up with an answer of their own. The nature of the middle-class revolutions in Germany and Italy during the 1930's is not an encouraging thing to consider in this context. By 1984 the threat to American democracy may not be an external one from Communism but rather an internal one from a native American revolution of the Right. The insecurities and frustrations of suburban life can provide a fertile field for such a growth. Resentments and anxieties being stored up today might explode with terrible power in the next two or three decades. Barricades in Park Forest or Levittown might seem unlikely, but history has produced some unlikely events.

Disaster is by no means inevitable. Men may solve the social problems which information technology is going to bring. Ethical and sociological progress will have to be rapid if it is to catch up with the computers; but such progress can be made. However, on the basis of our past performances in attempting to keep human development in pace with technological change, we have little reason to be optimistic. If suburban man has not yet learned to solve the dilemma of good and evil caused by industrialism, there is certainly no reason to expect that he will do much better in facing the mixed blessings of electronic decision-making.

V. The Suburban Apostolate

The problem of the "revival" is one of taking advantage of a mood to enlist people in a cause which, if successful, will then destroy the mood. . . . You can't have even a half-souled revival without some people becoming revived. Prophets will yet appear in the suburbs. Hard sayings will yet ring out over the green fields of Westchester County. . . .

JOHN COGLEY, in *The Commonweal*

Liturgy, Social Action, personal spiritual development—these have long been taken to be the foundations of the Apostolate. In this concluding section we devote one chapter to the problems of the liturgical movement in modern America and one to the new forms of Social Action. It is in these two fields that Catholic suburbanites have great challenges and great opportunities. The third chapter deals with the personal spiritual resources a suburbanite should bring to his apostolic effort, and the concluding chapter attempts to define the essence of the suburban problem.

18
Popular Culture and the Roman Rite

When the liturgical movement was confined to a few abbeys, a couple of schools and a handful of brave parishes, it enjoyed certain strategic advantages. It could promise remarkable results if its suggestions were adopted, without being forced to offer too much in the way of concrete proof. But now that it has attained a moderate success and is spreading with some speed to more and more parishes, it is frequently called on to explain what certain critics think are failures of its promises.

No one could legitimately expect that a few dialogue or sung Masses would turn a parish into a living community; but even in those parishes where a rather full liturgical program is in operation, the "living parish" still seems in the far distant future.

In this essay I intend to examine one of the obstacles which prevent the liturgical revival from realizing its full potential. This obstacle is the vast cultural gap between the Roman liturgy as a means of expression and communication and the industrial culture of urban America.

In his thought-provoking *Patterns in Comparative Religion* Mircea Eliade hints at the basic reason for this gap.[1] He observes that the fundamental religious intuitions of the human race have not changed since the most primitive times. These insights may at different times in history have been elevated or depraved, they may have been set in vastly different contexts, but their essential content has remained substantially the same.

Thus the notions of the creating father in the heavens, the regenerative powers of water, the rever-

[1] New York: Sheed & Ward, 1958.

ence due to sacred places, the importance of sacred times (especially the recurring year) —these appear in virtually all religions. (Of course the men of faith see in these themes a providential preparation of all peoples for the revealed religion, and believe that whatever Christian use was made of them was no more than a purifying and elevation of what was good in natural religion.)

On reading Eliade's chapters one cannot but be struck by two things: first, the remarkable manner in which the liturgy has employed these fundamental intuitions to a machine culture. Most of the basic religious insights Eliade lists are closely connected with the world of nature, were conceived by men who lived very close to nature, and can best be understood by men who are in tune with nature. In other words, man's religion through the ages has been primarily a religion closely connected with rural and agricultural activities, even when centered in a city. But the inhabitants of *modern* urban centers are independent of the forces of nature and of agricultural and pastoral processes to a degree that was unthinkable in Rome, Athens, Babylon or even medieval Paris. Nature has little influence on their lives, at least little that they immediately perceive.

Thus, rain is no longer the bearer of new life to the fields; it is something that can ruin a picnic in the countryside. The cold of winter does not represent very clearly a symbolic death, but it does make the commuter trains run less regularly and necessitates anti-freeze in the family car. Spring is not so much a rebirth as a time for the substitution of screens for storm windows. Thunder does not bring to mind the anger of the gods, but simply the failure of the weather forecaster.

An incident during my seminary days brought this home very forcefully to me. Our music teacher used to protest that city boys could not possibly understand fully the paschal lamb theme of the Holy Week liturgy unless they knew from personal experience the innocence and lovableness of a young lamb. It must be admitted that we thought his plan to import a lamb (along with its prize-winning mother) to the seminary at Easter time just a trifle odd. But when the seminarians bade a sad farewell to little Beppo after his two-week stay, they understood the Easter liturgy much better and were willing to admit that the imaginative professor might have had a point.

If one studies the Roman liturgy with an experience like this in mind one is appalled at the amount of material which can have little more than theoretical meaning for the modern city-dweller, whose scientific powers have immunized him almost completely from nature and the more elemental processes of maintaining human life. Heating and air-conditioning systems make the changing seasons much less noticeable than they were in the past and, it is to be feared, weaken considerably the subtle pedagogy of the liturgical year. In fact, it is difficult to think of anything more foreign to the liturgical cycle than the cycle of the secular year in our society. Both human religion and the Roman liturgy, in other words, came into being when mechanized urban living as we know it today was undreamed-of. Insofar as he is alienated from the world of nature, the city-dweller seems also to run the risk of being alienated from much of the meaning of the liturgy. He simply does not and cannot get its message.

If this were the full extent of the problem, the situation would be serious enough. But unfortunately it is much worse than would appear at first glance. Modern man's mental and emotional processes are not merely foreign to the type of world from which the Roman liturgy has sprung; they are to a great extent under the influence of forces which are diametrically opposed to the spirit of the liturgy. This becomes apparent if we compare the "sober and chaste rites" of the Roman liturgy with modern popular or mass culture.

For the sociologist, "mass culture" has a very precise meaning. It is "mass-produced" or "machine-made" amusement which is provided to offer diversion during the newly acquired leisure time of the urban working man. It belongs neither to the world of high culture, which élites have produced through the ages, nor to the world of folk culture, which has come up from the people of agricultural or pastoral civilizations. It is rather something which is produced for the urban mass by highly skilled professionals and purveyed to its purchasers by the mass media—radio, TV, magazines, newspapers, advertising billboards, etc. Thus the latest disk jockey favorite belongs neither to the world of Schubert nor the world of the folk ballad. It is the product of an entirely new cultural form and is, according to many, a depraved form.

This brings us to the essential contention of this chapter—that the emotional orientations of Christians in days gone by were formed by influences with which the liturgy was in tune, and that these influences have been replaced in our day by the mass media, which are to a great degree opposed to the spirit of the liturgy. The vast differences between the liturgy and our culture are evident enough; but there is some reason to explore them in detail since they are essential to our problem.

First of all, popular culture is basically sensual — it appeals primarily and chiefly to the senses. But since the senses are easily jaded if they are constantly excited by the same stimuli, mass culture must strive to produce ever stronger sensual effects. Screens get bigger, color gets brighter, sound gets louder and more pervasive. Vast technical skill is required to produce such effects and even greater skill is required to think up new ones.

However, the mass media are still managing to keep

one step ahead of themselves. Sometimes the results are a little odd. If you would like to have the roar of an African lion in your front room, your stereo-tape dealer will sell you a lion's roar which sounds more like the lion than does the lion himself.

Secondly, the mass media, since they have only passing contact with their audiences and indeed very little with the audiences' intellects, must strive to produce quick effects. Little time can be wasted on details; the plot situation, the song's theme, the joke's point, the advertiser's message—all must be got across quickly or be wasted. Hence the products of the mass media tend to be ephemeral. There is nothing more out-of-date than last year's top comedian or last year's top Florida hotel.

Since it is ephemeral, there is little opportunity for mass culture to have more depth. Even when it tries to deal with serious problems, it usually oversimplifies or even distorts them. The mass media can urge us to go to the "church of our choice" on Sunday, but do not dare offer much in the way of reasons for this advice.

There is also little room for variety. Once a plot line or a successful formula is found, it must be used over and over again. Hence we find the TV channels crowded with situation comedies or serious westerns or quiz shows, depending on what the current fad seems to be. Short stories in the slick magazines vary little from issue to issue. The mark of a successful writer for this medium is the ability to tell the same story in many different ways.

The reasons for such monotonous standardizations are mainly financial. Most efforts of the mass media are extremely expensive to produce. It is bad business to experiment too much when you have a successful formula.

Finally mass culture has little use for symbols. Its advertising branch is currently interested in creating a kind of symbol in "brand personalities" (e.g. the Marlboro man), but the approach is always direct rather than symbolic. There seems little point in using a symbol for a beer can when a picture of the can itself is just as easy to obtain. The mass media rarely find it wise to leave anything to their audience's imaginations.

Eliade's observation that "thanks chiefly to his symbols, the real existence of primitive man was not the broken and alienated existence lived by civilized man today" would not have much meaning to the manufacturers of popular culture.

It takes but a moment's thought to see how different is the spirit of the Roman liturgy, "with its grand simplicity, its sobriety hostile to all exuberance, fully matter of fact, speaking . . . without pretense or vanity or doubt or *hybris*." Where popular culture is sensual, the liturgy is restrained; where popular culture achieves its effect quickly, the liturgy works slowly and subtly. Where popular culture is ephemeral, direct and standardized, the liturgy is profound, indirect and symbolic. The two seem to be products of totally different types of civilization. It is no wonder that Father H. A. Reinhold speaks of the "strangeness of the Roman liturgy"; he might well have said "foreignness."

Popular culture is an obstacle to the liturgy as a means of communication and expression only to the extent that such culture forms the emotional and psychological orientations of the people who are exposed to it. I know of no studies indicating the full degree of the influence of mass culture on the mentality of Americans. (There have been surveys in limited areas, however; one example is a book purporting to show a connection between comic books and juvenile delinquency.) It seems safe to presume, nevertheless, that the influence is not inconsiderable. Let us think of the boy who spends his Saturday afternoon reading

comic books and his Saturday evening watching such
choice tidbits as "Gunsmoke," "Witch Doctor" and
"Purple People Eater" on Your Hit Parade, and then,
"I Was a Teen-age Monster from Outer Space" on
Shock Theatre. Such a lad may find it just a little
hard to get very much out of Mass the following
morning.

Nor can a group of teen-aged girls who spend several hours every afternoon staring goggle-eyed at
"American Bandstand" get excited over an Easter
Vigil. Neither will their male friends who, when
driving in a car, station one of their number at the
radio controls to assure that the current "top ten"
headliner will be heard over and over again. Indeed,
most Americans seem incapable of riding in a car
without having a radio playing loudly. Adults whose
world-view is shaped by the sports page, the death
notices, and the latest issue of *Life* or the *Saturday
Evening Post* will more than likely find that a dialogue
Mass is so novel as to "interfere with their prayers."

Obviously one could go on. The precise size of the
obstacle which mass culture presents to the liturgy
might be in question; but that it is a rather large
obstacle scarcely seems to require further proof.

There are, in theory at least, four solutions to the
problem — the maintenance of the status quo, the
abandonment of modern civilization, the complete
change of the liturgy, or some combination of the last
two. By definition the liturgical apostolate must reject the first solution. The second course, however,
has proved attractive to many within the movement.
Conrad Pepler's recent little book *Riches Despised*
urges just that course. True liturgy, it is argued, is
so foreign to machine civilization that the two can
never be reconciled.

This seems an unduly pessimistic view. A Church
which claims to be catholic can hardly abandon a
whole civilization which has been centuries in the

building and which has brought many unquestionable benefits (along with not a few evils) to the human race. The agricultural and pastoral religions had their beauty, one must admit; but one need only glance through a few pages of Eliade to see that peasant worship can become corrupt without any help from the big cities. In the practical order, furthermore, it seems rather unlikely that any sizable groups of people are going to give up the comfort — and the intellectual facilities — of the big city for the dubious promises of the simple life. Nor can we expect much from an attempt to bring the liturgy somehow into harmony with modern civilization and its mass culture. The Church is not going to abandon two thousand years of tradition to suit the moods of the habitual TV viewer or the comic book addict.

The only practical course which remains is to change modern civilization while at the same time modifying the liturgy. Such a solution will not satisfy those who like simple answers, but it seems to be the course which the Holy See has adopted: on the one hand, it insists on the need for social reform and, on the other, authorizes considerable changes in the liturgy for "pastoral" reasons. The process of this twofold change will of necessity be slow, but there seems to be no other way.

There are two final points that could be made. First of all, it seems that one of the objectives of a change in modern civilization would be to bring more of the country to the city (much as our music professor did, though in a more sophisticated way), or at least to preserve some of the country in the expanding city. Thus liturgists might find that such an "alien" field as city planning is an essential area of study if they are to achieve their goals.

Secondly, can we not pose at least the theoretical question as to whether a few of the best elements of popular culture could not be, somehow or other, integrated into the liturgy? Is there some way that the assimilation of the popular hymnody of the Middle Ages could be repeated (not necessarily in the area of song)? The marriages between modern architecture and liturgy and between modern polyphony and plain chant prove that at least some elements in modern civilization are not necessarily foreign to the spirit of the liturgy.

This has been a theoretical essay. I do not wish to be accused of putting obstacles in the way of liturgical participation. I do not advocate that the sung and dialogue Masses shall wait till every family has a flock of sheep grazing on their front lawn. But as the liturgical movement matures, it would seem that it should be able to devote at least a little time to thoughtful consideration of some problems which are larger than its immediate day-to-day program.

19
The New
Social Action

It is just possible that, as thought begins to crystal-
lize on the nature of America's new and post-war economic problems, the papal principles of *Quadragesimo
Anno* will be seen to have as much validity as they had
in 1938, albeit in a different framework of problems.
It is possible, indeed, that Catholic Social Action, now
looking for new directions, might find an application
of the principles of *Quadragesimo Anno* to the new
economic problems would afford fruitful insights and
perhaps even the suggestion of several new practical
programs.

One cannot but think these thoughts as he ponders
the future role of the Church; he cannot but think of
the Church as he ponders the recent two-volume report of the Committee on Economic Development,
Problems of United States Economic Development.
The report is a symposium of ninety-nine essays sub-
mitted by various economists and near-economists in
answer to the question "What is the most important
economic problem to be faced by the United States in
the next twenty years?" Although the answers cover a
vast range of problems, most of these seem to have
fallen into five classes—foreign aid, economic stability
(which for most of the writers meant inflation), urban
congestion, the deterioration of the public sector of the
economy, and the absence of economic goals and
values in an age of relative abundance. Each of the
problems is staggeringly large and frighteningly complex, and seems to admit of no solution unless there is
general co-operation among the many competing
giants of the American political economy.

A free society is at a distinct disadvantage in the

planning of broad objectives. Once a consensus is reached on a goal a free society normally makes rapid progress toward the goal. But the many competing and countervailing forces within the society reach a consensus on the answer to—or even the existence of—a problem only after slow and painful deliberation. An authoritarian economy is under no such disadvantage; it can move with all the initial efficiency of the ant hill. The free society can count on the long-run merits of free co-operation to give it the edge in competition with the slave state; unfortunately this long run may well turn out to be, in the present world situation, the long run of Lord Keynes in which we shall all be dead. Thus a free society is forced today to find new institutions for the obtaining of a consensus or perish—either by destruction from without or strangulation from within. The principles of economic organization given by Pius XI can well inspire the promotion of such institutions.

A consensus on foreign aid seems remote. Americans are vaguely aware that the rich nations of the world are getting richer and the poor are getting poorer. They seem to realize that the exploding population in Asia and Africa is far outstripping the industrial expansion of these so-called uncommitted peoples. They may even sense that the seeming wonders of Russian industry can appear extremely attractive to a nation living on the brink of starvation. But there seems little disposition to devote the needed one per cent of our national income to foreign development, much less to contribute such money to some independent international development organization which would not be under the control of the American Congress. An effective foreign aid program would require a vast co-ordination of tariff policy, agricultural surplus programs, business investment, and labor and management participation. An institution which would enable the various economic giants of our country to form such a program, publicize it, and press for its implementation is nonexistent. Without the co-operation of the different "veto groups" the government will not be able to act. Our miserable showing to date is proof of this. Foreign aid will continue to be a political football, and the average taxpayer will heave a sigh of relief when his Congressman forbids the Chief Executive to "pour any more money down the drain."

About the only consensus on inflation is that it is a bad thing and someone — someone else, of course — ought to do something about it. The experts and the general public are in disagreement as to whether it is a traditional "demand" inflation or a new kind of "cost-price" inflation or a combination of both. Nor is there agreement as to who must bear the blame; the various economic groups insist that they are acting in the only way they possibly can. So the three per cent annum inflation continues, and we are told that this, with the suffering it involves for many of our fixed-income groups, is the necessary price of progress. One might be permitted to remark that such a solution has about it a vaguely familiar ring.

Foreign economic policy and domestic stability are not particularly new problems although the shape they take today is quite new. But the difficulties caused by the tremendous expansion of metropolitan regions are quite new and hence much farther from solution. The unplanned and impetuous sprawl of Suburbia, Exurbia, and Interurbia threatens to turn our nation into one great slum devoid of adequate transportation, of natural beauty, of recreational facilities, of breathable air and potable water, or even fairly efficient utilities, and of decent cultural equipment. The huge metropolitan strips stretching for hundreds of miles and containing tens of millions of people will make the cities of the 1930's and the 1940's seem pleasant places indeed. We are told that it will cost at least two trillion dollars for our cities to be kept for the next two decades as habitable as they are today—and this quite apart from any thought of improving them. The suburban migration which seemed to be the answer to many an American's dream is rapidly becoming a national nightmare.

Urban planners maintain that the problem is not a lack of technical skills in city development or even a lack of financial resources; rather they tell us that the cause of urban congestion is largely a breakdown of the metropolitan governmental system. City government has become inadequate, makeshift, obsolete. Within the emergent metropolitan regions there are literally hundreds of jealous and competing sovereignties—national, state, county and local. In the New York Metropolitan Region there are over one thousand independent governmental units, in Chicago more than nine hundred. Small wonder that there is administrative chaos and almost no effective planning. If foreign aid and the prevention of inflation require institutions for co-operation among the private sectors of our political economy, urban congestion requires an institution for the co-operation of the different public sectors. Nor can labor, business and farm groups be left out of such an institution. The construction industry—both employer and labor groups—must take their share of responsibility; and big business will have to learn that it has more obligations to an urban region than the paying of taxes on a new suburban factory. Once again, however, we look in vain for institutions which would make such co-operation possible on a large scale. (Although the work done by business interests in Pittsburgh indicates that this co-operation is by no means impossible.)

Closely connected with urban congestion — indeed one of the causes of it—is the breakdown in public services. But it would seem that the world's richest nation cannot afford efficient public services. As J. K. Galbraith puts it in the C.E.D. report:

The newspapers day-by-day . . . chronicle our increased output of goods—of automobiles, electronic entertainment, human plumage, bedevilling surpluses of food, and the myriads of other blessings and preoccupations. But the same papers tell us just as urgently of our poverty in other things. They tell of the shortages of schools, the shortage of teachers, the inability of police and welfare workers to deal with juvenile crime, the failure of sanitation service to keep abreast of the litter from the increasingly elaborate packages in which our products come. . . . A millionaire who has six Cadillacs, a superb cigarette lighter, and an admirably caparisoned wife is not really well off if his children have no school and he must live with them in a chicken coop.

There is no reason why a community should not seek to satisfy its public needs with the same vigor and enthusiasm and the same sense of achievement and gratification that it views its satisfaction of private wants. The building of schools is not inherently inferior to the production of television sets. The building of roads is not inherently inferior to the building of cars that use them.

There is indeed no reason except that there exist no institutions effectively to champion the improvement of government services except the beleaguered executive branches of government. No one doubts the need for better schools, but one can question whether education will keep pace with our needs, much less improve, if there is not some national organization of the various sectors in our economy which depend on the educational system and which are willing to co-operate in improving it.

The question of goals is of course the most important one the C. E. D. report raises, and the one which most needs a co-operative framework to be answered. In a free society goals cannot be arrived at by fiat from above; nor can they be reached by simple majority vote. They are rather the result of constant communication and co-operation, of day-by-day exchange of ideas and interaction of personnel. Such co-operation and interaction are by no means absent from our society. But they are often stunted and maimed by bitter conflicts which are many times unnecessary. (One shudders to think of the harm to labor management co-operation that the unfortunate "right to work" campaign has caused.) In a time of relative abundance and even affluence no single group can decide even in general what direction our tremendously productive economy should take. There was less difficulty when there was a depression to be mastered or a war to be won. But now the economy continues to grind out an ever increasing stream of ever more fancy gadgets while a good part of the human race faces starvation, while a minority of our own people live in unnecessary poverty, and while our education and other public services rapidly deteriorate.

One cannot but think of the words of Pius XII in the encyclical *Le Pèlerinage de Lourdes,* where he condemns a materialism which "rages in a love of money, which creates even greater havoc as modern enterprises expand and which . . . determines many of the decisions which weigh heavy on the life of the people. It finds expression in the cult of the body, in excessive desire for comforts and in flight from all the austerities of life . . . it shows itself in a lack of interest in one's brother, in selfishness which crushes him, in justice which deprives him of his life . . . a concept of life which regulates everything in terms of material prosperity and earthly satisfaction."

Should Americans apply this condemnation to themselves, or should they rather find comfort in Professor Maritain's recent book wherein he said that

Americans were not materialists but rather used material things to bring about human freedom and happiness? Or perhaps both the Pope and Maritain describe the American political economy accurately but from different viewpoints. The American people by and large may not be more selfish than any other, more materialistic than any other. In fact, they have in certain areas a wonderful record for generosity (community fund drives and the like). Could it not be rather that Americans are hampered by outmoded institutions which force the nation to take a selfish pose that no longer represents the spirit of the people (if it ever did)? Is it not possible that the absence of institutions of intergroup co-operation restricts and restrains the dynamic altruism which is at least part of the basis of the American experiment?

If such a hunch is correct, Catholic Social Actionists are in an excellent strategic position. It should not be too difficult to apply the principles of *Quadragesimo Anno* to the situation and come up with the beginnings of an extremely constructive answer. It would not be labeled a "Papal Plan," but would rather stand on its own merits. Could not, for example, Catholics begin to suggest a series of national intergroup conferences on our major economic problems, conferences which would not only study the causes of problems but would also have some authority to implement solutions? The White House Conference on Education of several years ago sets up some sort of precedent, though we would perhaps expect more of a "follow-through" from future conferences. Obviously such a program presupposes political leadership which will not pull the rug out from under its own recommendations, but any program must make such a presupposition.

It would be naïve and unrealistic to think that the lion and the lamb—or rather a whole group of lions— are going to lie together in peace and harmony. Conflict and competition will continue, nor are they necessarily evil in the free society. Group co-operation on larger problems affecting the common good is not a magic formula; nor is it the ultimate solution to a problem. Rather it is only the beginning of rational discussion. But such a beginning must be made and made soon. Those of us who believe in the timeless value of the fundamental principles of Catholic Social Action would perhaps do well to dust off our tattered copies of *Quadrageismo Anno* and see if it still has something to say, even in an age of affluence.

20

A Spirituality
for Suburbanites

The basic principles of the Christian life have changed remarkably little since they were first announced on Galilean hillsides and by the shores of the Lake of Genesareth almost two thousand years ago. The love of God and the love of neighbor are still the greatest of the commandments and still the most difficult. Christian spirituality is still essentially the growth in the virtue of charity. Charity, however, is more than a vague sentimental sympathy with the poor and the unfortunate. Before the will can love, the intellect must know, and before it can love well it must acquire discipline. The lesser virtues which cluster around charity help man to know how to love and to develop the strength of will to love as he should. Charity does not change, but the ways in which it must be exercised can vary from age to age. The intellectual preparation for Christian love is different in different eras, and the forces contrary to love against which the Christian will must discipline itself are not the same in each century.

Hence in these days of renewed interest in the spiritual life there have appeared on the scene a wide variety of "spiritualities"—for married people, for single people, for diocesan priests, for doctors, for workers, for intellectuals. Actually these "spiritualities" are nothing more than the application of the traditional principles of Christian asceticism to the new problems and new spiritual environment of our time—a task which is not always easy. One hesitates to enter this already confused arena of "spiritualities" with a new contestant. Indeed the very words "spirituality for suburbanites" are enough to make a good many people choke (with laughter, one hopes, instead of rage). Nevertheless it would be improper for a priest writing a collection of essays on the suburbs to omit a chapter which would contain at least some attempt to indicate how the spiritual problems of the new middle class might be solved.

As was indicated in an earlier chapter, the most obvious of the spiritual difficulties in suburban life is the apparent conflict between the necessity of detachment and the material affluence of our consumption-orientated society. Every suburban home is full of gadgets, some of them even paid for, and the parade of gimmicks is not likely to end. American science may be behind the Russians' in rocket technology, but it is nonetheless busy turning out such marvels as an ultrasonic dishwasher that knocks off the dirt with sound waves, an electronic hostess cart that can be wheeled to any part of the house or yard and keep dishes hot or cold, a baby bottle cooler and warmer with a clock attachment that warms the bottle again if the baby isn't hungry when the alarm sounds.

Not only do gadgets service us in our household needs, they amuse us in our leisure time. The amount of money spent in Florida on deep-sea fishing is greater than the combined grosses of the state's citrus and cattle industries. In St. Louis, Missouri, there are more pleasure boats registered with the U. S. Coast Guard than there are in Boston. Michigan last year licensed sixty-one thousand people to hunt with bow and arrow.

The economics behind this fantastic accumulation of gadgets and pleasures are startling. Of our four hundred thirty-five billion dollar national income, something like a hundred billion dollars is being spent on things people really don't need, things beyond the basic necessities of living such as food, clothing, housing, transportation, medical expenses, insurance.

These gadgets are not evil; they represent man's continued ordering of the forces of nature over which God has given him dominion. But the human tendency to greed being what it is, one might ask whether the eye of the needle through which we rich Americans must pass on our way to salvation is not becoming cluttered. Perhaps the affluent society is on its way to becoming the avaricious society.

Therefore one of the prime requisites for a suburban spiritual life must be mortification. The necessity of self-denial is not a particularly new discovery in the history of Christian asceticism, but one wonders if it could ever have been more necessary than it is in our gadget-ridden culture. If the suburbanite is to use his gadgets instead of being used by them, if he is to be their master instead of their slave, then he must put in his life rigorous, consistent, and carefully planned mortification. To use his gadgets properly he must deny himself some of them. To enjoy them in the most fully human as well as the Christian fashion, he must deliberately detach himself from some of them—in the words of T. S. Eliot, he must learn to care and not to care.

One might well question whether there is much voluntary mortification in the suburbs. It is certainly not obvious. The only real limitation of spending seems to be the size of discretionary income or the availability of consumer credit. Few people seem to see much point in depriving themselves of anything which they think they can afford—at least as long as some money has been put aside for the precious college education of offspring. The American consumer may not be quite as stupid as the automobile designers and motivation research men thought, but there is little doubt that he wants more, more, more.

The problem is not made easier by the fact that no one is able to advise the rare suburbanite who is looking for ways of mortification as to precisely what he should give up. It is easy, of course, to suggest that a Pontiac will serve the purpose as well as a Cadillac and the difference could be given to the poor, but such advice is only a beginning. Self-denial, to be effective, requires more than occasional spectacular acts of generosity. It must become a way of life; it must involve a continuing series of decisions which no one except the members of a family can make. It may be one of the greatest agonies of life in the world—one not shared by those in the religious state—that these decisions never come to an end. There can never be a rule giving precise regulations for this kind of poverty. It is to be hoped that a literature will grow up which will spell out a little more clearly what poverty of spirit should mean in an age of abundance. Such a literature would be a great help to people living in an affluent society and at the same time trying to follow the way of poverty, but it would not release them from the obligation of personal decisions.

A close cousin of mortification is generosity. As was indicated in another chapter, Americans are not an avowedly greedy people; they do not pile up possessions merely for the sake of ownership. Quite the contrary; financial generosity is a definite American virtue. There are few noble causes which will not impel an average suburbanite to reach for his checkbook, especially if the cause is well-organized and well-advertised. One need not be too enthusiastic about his generosity. Some of it might be salve for guilt feelings; some of it might be motivated by community pressure. Who would turn down the Community Chest or the March of Dimes? Nevertheless, the financial generosity of the modern middleclass American is real and much of it is not without its merit.

But financial generosity is not enough. God does not necessarily find sacrifices and burnt-offerings pleasing unless they come from a humble heart. God wants more than that we give part of what we own;

He wants us. Thus the man who "has" must be generous also with himself. He can be neither beat nor cool. He must give himself to works of active charity or active social justice. He must not let himself grow blind to the miseries of the world beyond his secluded little bastion. He must devote part of his life to the personal service of the least of Christ's brothers.

Again, no one can tell him precisely what form this *engagement* must take. To be effective it will normally have to be organized. It might concern itself with direct charity, as the St. Vincent de Paul Society of Frederick Ozanam did and in many ways still does. There are still the hungry to be fed and sick to be visited even in the welfare state. Or his commitment might be to the larger social problems which metropolitan development brings. Or he might dedicate himself to building the community of Christ which his parish should be; he could promote the active liturgy, or the Confraternity classes for public school children or the various Catholic Action groups. He might do any of these things or others, but he must do something or he is scarcely worthy of being called a Christian.

There are few more encouraging signs in American Catholicism than the recent interest in the limited-service lay missionary movements such as the Association for International Development. Organizations such as these may well be the salvation of the Church in the suburbs. A parish with five or ten people who had spent two years in missionary work in New Guinea or Brazil or the Congo would almost certainly have a spirit different from that of a parish where consciousness of the catholicity of the Church was dim. Such a missionary sense seems to be desperately needed. Without it there is little of that sense of urgency on which personal generosity depends.

In the chapter on suburban leisure, it was stated that good taste was required if suburban leisure was not to turn into a nightmare of TV westerns, mass-produced short stories and stereophonic Rock and Roll. But good taste is more than a mere norm for the use of leisure; in a society where there is so much leisure and so many ways of spending and wasting time, it becomes a fundamental principle of the spiritual life. Actually, this is nothing more than an application to modern life of the often misunderstood virtue of prudence, a virtue whose effect is not to restrain us from acting or to confine us to what has always been done, but rather to guide us to what ought to be done now.

If time is not to be wasted, if opportunities are to be seized, if intellects are to be developed, emotions balanced and wills strengthened, then in our confused and noisy society, considerable amounts of prudence—exercised in good taste—are essential. It should not be too difficult to see that listening to an FM radio instead of an AM might bring a person closer to God or provide more of the raw material for spiritual development. Satirist Mort Sahl has speculated as to whether disk jockeys or used car salesmen are more useless to society, but there can be no debate as to which of the two is more of an obstacle to the spiritual progress of teen-agers (with apologies to all of the disk jockeys with taste and used car salesmen with consciences).

The ways of training in good taste are beyond the scope of this essay. It suffices to say that both the mortification of saying "no" to trash and the generosity exercised in spending time on those things which cultivated men have considered beautiful are needed. However, no young suburbanite is likely to be impressed with Tolstoy or Woolf when his father never gets beyond Perry Mason and westerns, or to become familiar with Mozart and Stravinsky if his mother is never interested in listening to anything.

A fourth area of suburban spiritual development

would be a growing awareness of the obligation of educated people to read. Msgr. George Higgins has said, "The biggest single need of the American Church is more lay people who read." The reasons should be obvious. One will not be a good apostle if one does not think. One will normally not think unless one is exposed to new ideas outside one's own particular field; and the best (in many cases the only) source of new ideas is reading. Granted that more Catholics are reading good books than ever before, granted too that suburbanite Catholics are doing better than most others, still the fact remains that most Catholics, suburban as well as urban and rural, simply do not read, or at least do not read nearly as much as they could or should. In fact, considering the rise in the level of education, a good case might be made for the assertion that the ratio of reading to education is declining. It is terrifying to think that young men and women can graduate from college and become financially successful not only without being able to write good English but without even the desire to read good English. Far too many suburbanites, Catholic or not, are only semi-literate, despite their college degrees.

Since we are concerned with the spiritual life, the necessity for the more directly spiritual books should receive first mention. Although the body of literature on spiritual problems for lay people is not yet altogether satisfactory, it is rapidly improving and growing.[3] Furthermore, the obligations of the Christian life are not limited to matters that are directly spiritual. Reading on the secular problems which face the community and the Church is also something of a duty for the Christian who is seeking perfection. Who could say that in the late 1950's books on the race problem do not have spiritual implications for the Christian layman?

Closely connected with (and perhaps in some cases a substitute for) reading are the adult education movements which are rapidly increasing in urban centers. University extensions, Great Books discussion groups, World Politics forums, Catholic organizations like Chicago's Adult Education Centers, study groups within existing organizations, parish forums and lecture series—all these are helping to promote respect for the things of the intellect and the spirit in the big cities and their suburban satellites. They may not have had a major impact on suburban life as yet, but at least they destroy the excuse that nothing is available for the suburbanite who is looking for something more serious than the latest issue of *Time*.

Mortification, generosity, good taste, intellectual curiosity—these are some of the possible staples of a spiritual program for suburbanites. They are dignified and appealing virtues; no one need feel apologetic for recommending them. Other virtues could be explored. What do chastity and obedience mean for married people in our society? How can the presence of God be practiced while one is involved in the Busy Life? Is contemplation possible in our "mink-lined rat traps"? Do we trust in God as we should? What kinds of popular devotions are suited to modern needs? These are important questions. But there is one more important; indeed it is the basic question of modern spirituality for lay people—or perhaps it has always been basic: How does one persuade the laity that sanctity is for them too, that holiness is the vocation of all, that being an average Catholic means being a mediocre follower of Christ? To be ordinary in the love of God and neighbor is not enough—for the disciples of Christ. It never has been and it never will be.

21
Conclusion

The reader who has struggled through these chapters has by now no doubt come to the conclusion that the author is an ambivalent in his reactions as the people he is describing. He has alternately criticized Suburbia and defended it against the attacks of other critics. In reality, however, one need not take sides. Attacking or defending the suburbs is rather like attacking or defending the weather—a waste of time. There are good things in suburban living and bad things; which will dominate in the future depends entirely on the free-will decisions of human beings.

There have been three main themes running through these essays—that Suburbia is the result of a partial flight from the physical and psychological evils of industrial society, that it represents an attempt to recapture the benefits of the primary group communities which industrialism has weakened if not destroyed, and that the suburbs offer a whole new set of problems — and opportunities — for the Catholic Church.

Suburbia represents a new humanism, an attempt to build as perfect an earthly paradise as is possible. It is not an atheist humanism like that of Karl Marx, but it is definitely a secularist humanism in that, for all the lip service paid to the Divinity, religion does not have much practical influence in its techniques or goals.

In this paradise all the available resources of modern technology are to be put to the service of human comfort and happiness. Drudgery, monotony, ugliness are to vanish from human life. Leisure will be at the disposal of everyone. Each family will be secure within itself and integrated into an active, exciting community. The price of such a humanist paradise will not be high. Suburbia will not demand a renouncing of freedom; there will be no dictatorships of the organization man. America's new capitalism will produce better results than those promised by Marxist humanism without requiring the slavery which Marxism seems to imply. Mankind has at last emerged from the dark ages of misery and insecurity. The suburbs are the final proof that the marriage between technology and democracy has been a happy and successful one.

Such is the vision of suburban humanism. Let us not underestimate its power. Suburbia does indeed offer more material comfort to a greater number of people than ever before in man's existence. This is no small accomplishment. Material comfort is not everything in life, but neither is it to be rejected completely. It is a manifestation of man's mastery over the irrational forces of the universe and, as such, part of God's creative plan. Nor is Suburbia content with mere material satisfactions. In its emphasis on domesticity and community it seeks also to meet basic spiritual needs. It may not pay too much attention to God in its daily life, yet the tremendous suburban religious revival has certainly assigned God a place of dignity and honor (if not of influence) in suburban culture.

Yet Suburbia is not always happy. Leisure is not as much fun as it promised to be; time weighs heavily and yet goes too fast. Life is full of activity and yet curiously devoid of significance. People have "never had it so good," yet look back with longing to times gone by. Families do more things together, yet husband and wife, parents and children, often feel that they are living with strangers. The neighborhoods are scenes of active, even frantic, participation; yet resentment, envy and feuding is rift. Success has been achieved, yet is still slipping through fingers. Security is always just around the corner. There never seems to be any time to rest or to relax or to enjoy life. Material comforts are on all sides, yet there is so little opportunity to enjoy them. Everyone is educated, yet almost everyone is confused. "Good times" abound, yet something seems to be missing. Everyone strives to be well-adjusted, yet the community is as maladjusted as ever. People lead reasonably good lives and yet feel uncomfortably guilty.

What could be the cause of so much guilt feeling? . . . . [it is caused by] man's own conscience; he senses his gifts of talents, his ability to love, to think, to laugh, to cry, to wonder and to create; he senses that his life is the one chance he is given; and that if he loses this chance he has lost everything. He lives in a world with more comfort and ease than his ancestors ever knew, yet he senses that, chasing after more comfort, his life runs through his fingers like sand. He cannot help but feel guilty for the waste, the lost chance."[1] So Fromm the agnostic sees that, for all his comforts, suburban man is not happy, because he has lost sight of the good, the true and the beautiful. He has tried to retreat from the human race into his own comfortable little bailiwick and ignore the sufferings and struggles of the rest of humanity. The materialism of the suburbs may not be wrong in itself, but it can never satisfy the deeper longings of the human heart until it begins to transcend its own narrowness. Suburbia's sins of commission may be few, but its sins of omission are many.

To the agnosticism of Fromm, the Christian must add the concept of the Mystical Body, a doctrine which is mentioned often in Suburbia but whose implications are not always understood. As far as observable religious practice goes, the Catholics of the suburbs are doing a splendid job, but the narrowness of their world-view is hard to reconcile either with

[1] Erich Fromm, *The Art of Loving* (New York: Harper, 1956).

the perfection of the Christian life or the vocation of an apostolic layman. The real tragedy of many a suburban Catholic is not that he is bad, but that he is capable of so much more good.

We must not, however, be too severe. Changes in attitude do not take place overnight. Suburban humanism is quite new for most people. It will take time for them to see its imperfections. John Cogley, who could scarcely be accused of being a wild admirer of the middle class, observes in *The Commonweal:*

> The intense young Catholics of today hold their meetings not in slum buildings but in ranch-type suburban homes. The emphasis has shifted from the working apostolate to the family movement. Great discussions used to be held over coffee or beer in the skid-row restaurant with the zealous curate finding his pressed suit an embarrassment. But in the long run, the discussions around a fireplace in a split-level home with the curate looking like a man who belongs there may actually be as meaningful . . . clearly a new day has dawned. The sun now rises over Larchmont, not Mott Street. The new generation of Catholics was not born on farming communes as Peter Maurin hoped they would be, but in the overcrowded maternity hospitals of a thousand suburbs. And here is where the Church's future lies. The Catholic College student who marched in the picket lines during the early days of the CIO, whether he knew it or not, was helping to build Park Forest and Levittown.

(And we might add, may well live in either of these suburbs along with the sons of the CIO workers and perhaps even some AFL-CIO organizers.)

If one interested in the spread of Christ's kingdom may find some cause for anxiety in suburbanism, there is as yet no reason for despair and there is perhaps some reason for bright expectations. Suburbia is a vast and rapidly growing land of enchantment; it is a maze, full of complexity and contradiction. One can find in it whatever one seeks. One observer sees a picture-windowed Babylon. John Cogley, on the other hand, sees a seed bed of future prophets. Both in a sense are right. Two beautiful worlds are growing up in the suburbs. One is the world of the gadget, the lovely world of color TV, deepfreezes, big hi-fis, two cars in the garage and tranquilizing drugs in the medicine cabinet. This world is not of itself bad. The other world is the world of the presumably spiritual: the world of the crowded churches, long lines at the Communion rail, CFM meetings, good will, and noble intentions. This world is not of itself enough. The basic trouble is that few suburbanites see any connection between the world of the gadget and the world of the spirit. It never occurs to them to ask whether there might not be some incongruity in the St. Christopher Medal and the Cadillac or the penitential ashes of Lent on the side of a Florida swimming pool. The intimate relationship between the Holy Eucharist and the new migrant in the heart of the city is not evident to them. They are not aware of the connection between their own abundance and starvation in India. It is to this basic secularism of Suburbia that the suburbanite prophet must address himself. If prophecy is indeed to be heard across the green fields of Westchester or DuPage Counties, it will be uttered by suburbanites in the language their fellows can understand. It will be spoken by people who know the culture from which they come, its strength and weakness, its goodness and its hesitancy and indecision, its fear and its false hopes, its great possibilities and its many failures.